Needlework Tools and Accessories

Needlework Tools and Accessories

A Collector's Guide

Molly G. Proctor

B.T. Batsford, London

ISBN 0 7134 5895 X

Typeset by Servis Filmsetting Ltd, Manchester
And printed by
The Bath Press, Bath

For the publishers
B.T. Batsford Limited
4 Fitzhardinge Street
London W1H 0AH

CONTENTS

JACKET ILLUSTRATIONS

Front: Child's needlework basket with contemporary packets of needles, crochet hook, stilleto, thimble, darner and sampler. Pin cube, German pattern book, Tunbridge Ware emery, Tartan Ware holder for packets of needles, cotton reels, bodkins, a mitrailleuse, tatting shuttles, scissors, needlecases, pincushions, glove darner, packet of boot buttons, knitting sheath, thread winders and stained ivory thimble case.

Back: Decorated box for cotton, cotton barrel, needlecases, thread winder, pincushions, sewing silk.

(Photography: Richard Bird)

ACKNOWLEDGEMENT

Most museums have some needlework tools and accessories in their collections; those used as a basis for this book are listed and I would like to thank their staff for helping me in various ways. Some had interesting and well-labelled displays on view, some suggested lines of research, others supplied valuable information in answer to my letters, and my particular gratitude goes to those museums that allowed me access to their reserve collections and freely gave me of their valuable time and specialist knowledge.

I would also like to thank several companies which responded so generously to my requests for information, in particular J. & P. Coats Ltd, Newey Goodman Ltd, Optilon Ltd, Sotheby's, Wedgwood Museum Trust, Wilkinson Sword Housewares Divison and William Briggs & Co. Ltd.

Valerie, Jean, Anne and Imogen very kindly allowed me to borrow items to be photographed and shared their knowledge of needlework tools with me.

Many of the illustrations were taken by museum photographers but I would like to thank Ronald White, Maidstone; Fotek, Bath; and David Clarke, Canterbury.

My thanks also to Emmie Shipman, who kindly improved my prose and spelling.

Special thanks are due to my husband who explained certain manufacturing processes to me; both he and my son listened attentively when asked and told me if they did not understand – men who know nothing about sewing are invaluable for such a task!

TABLE OF WEIGHTS AND MEASURES

Money

£ s d

2 farthings ($\frac{1}{4}$d)	=	1 halfpenny (ha'penny) ($\frac{1}{2}$d)
2 halfpennies	=	1 penny (1d)
12 pennies	=	1 shilling (1/-)
2 shillings and sixpence	=	half-a-crown (2/6d)
20 shillings	=	1 pound (£1)

Decimal

100 p = £1

Length

Imperial

12 inches	=	1 foot
3 feet	=	1 yard

Metric

1 metre = 1.094 yards

Cloth measure

$2\frac{1}{4}$ inches	=	1 nail
4 nails	=	1 quarter (9 in)
4 quarters	=	1 yard (36 in)
5 quarters	=	1 ell (45 in)

Miscellaneous

12 articles	=	1 dozen
12 dozen	=	1 gross
12 gross	=	1 great gross

INTRODUCTION

My interest in needlework tools developed out of research into the drapery trade between 1800 and 1950, therefore the emphasis in this book is on practical and inexpensive haberdashery which was sold in drapers' shops during this period.

I had the benefit of studying old catalogues from wholesale drapers and manufacturers which proved invaluable for identifying and dating everyday objects during this period. From these reliable sources, I discovered that many tools and accessories were sold over a very long period of time and continued to be manufactured much later than I had realized: for example, the use of a portrait of Queen Victoria on a label does not imply that it was made during her reign – some were still in use during the 1930s – nor is there truth in the widely-held belief that the nail became an obsolete unit of measurement before 1850, as in 1905 a shopkeeper could still buy a brass counter-measure calibrated with them.

From talking to the staff in some museums where there are specialist collections, and with the help of several old-established companies which manufacture sewing accessories, it seems probable there were two main reasons why some products were made without any alteration for so many years. First, as long as goods sold well some makers were reluctant to spend money on new packaging or improvements. Secondly, the perpetration of certain lines was a direct result of the large number of British people living overseas, who either ordered what they knew was satisfactory to be sent from home, or bought what they required from local shopkeepers, who in turn imported only what they knew they could sell.

Descriptions of the origins of the various subjects and their development to the mid eighteenth century are given here, but more information about this period can be found elsewhere and examples in museums are usually well-documented.

Changing social and economic situations, together with the increasing skill of the craftsmen from the late eighteenth century onwards, has resulted in an endless variety of decorative objects which delight the collector. Although not always practical, many of these charming or amusing novelties have been described and illustrated, but are not always easy to date accurately. Some originated in workboxes, which may be helpful, and the various firms which made souvenirs may have produced catalogues, but much reliance has to be put on methods of manufacture, availability of materials, fashion and a knowledge of contemporary antiques, which may be misleading as it was quite common for a good idea to be copied by another firm some time later.

Really old needlework tools are delightful, and a well-used piece has a charm of its own, but there is ample scope to collect and study the recent past, including examples made of plastic which may be a hundred years old already. There is much more to be discovered.

CHAPTER I

Needles

The craft of needlemaking was responsible for a primary tool of civilization. In the Stone Age, when man began to use skins for clothing, his first tool was probably made from the dried leaf of a yucca plant with the tip formed into a point and the shredded leaf used as thread. By 3000 BC needles made of bone were either pointed or shaped into a hook and during the Bronze Age bone needles had one to four eyes. Metal needles were introduced into Britain about 100 BC and from the Roman invasion to the Norman conquest it is probable all communities had craftsmen who made bronze needles and pins. Medieval wire workers were under the control of religious houses, and by the early sixteenth century there is evidence that steel needles were made in England at London, Dorchester, Colchester, Chichester, Chester, York, Hathersage, Much Wenlock, Kendal and Long Crendon; in Scotland at Sweetheart Abbey, Dumfries; and in Ireland at Limerick.

In the 1560s Queen Mary brought a Moor from Spain and established him in London as a needlemaker in an attempt to encourage the indigenous population, but he did not pass on his skills. However, when Elizabeth I offered religious tolerance to some Huguenots on condition they trained men to make fine needles, it was successful. By 1656 the needlemakers of London were powerful enough to obtain a Charter of Incorporation from Oliver Cromwell, The Arms of the Worshipful Company of Needlemakers have a Moor's head crest, supporters known as Adam and Eve with the woman holding a needle and three needles crowned on the shield. The Needlemakers' Hall stood on the site of the present Bank of England in Threadneedle Street, a name probably corrupted from 'three needles'. The Charter exhibited a most restrictive organization within a ten mile radius of the City of Westminster and, as a direct result, many craftsmen left London and settled elsewhere. Some migrated to the area around Studely and Redditch, on the borders of Warwickshire and Worcestershire, where needlemaking has remained the staple industry for nearly three hundred years. By the mid eighteenth century other centres of manufacture found they could not match the Redditch prices and one by one they closed, the last being at Long Crendon, Buckinghamshire, in 1860.

Until the Industrial Revolution, needlemaking was a cottage

industry. Members of a family were supplied with the raw material and tools by a merchant who collected and sold the finished article. Needles were expensive necessities – the Ratcliffe Greencoat School, Stepney, paid threepence each for them in 1757 – but towards the end of the eighteenth century some families began to specialize and became expert in one of the many operations, which slightly increased production and lowered the cost. 'Scouring' (polishing) needles by hand was a long and laborious process and the most important development in the industry was the adaptation of water mills for this purpose, which greatly increased production, improved quality and reduced costs. The skill and care applied to scouring in Redditch were responsible for its monopolizing needlemaking in Britain and, at its peak, supplying 90 per cent of the world market. Some of the largest factories made needles from start to finish, but there were a few specialists, including Forge Mill, Redditch, which just scoured needles. It was in production by 1730 but, contrary to some sources, there is no archaeological evidence of early needlemaking on the adjoining site of Bordesley Abbey. The mill continued to work until 1958 and is now the National Needle Museum, where the machinery for scouring may be seen in operation.

For nearly 200 years needlemaking remained virtually unchanged except for the introduction of machines to replace hand work. Wire came to a mill in coils of standard diameter and was brought to the correct gauge by drawing it through a series of holes of diminishing size. This was done by hand until 1850, but today's automated successor is capable of drawing wire at 100 mph. The wire was first cut into 'doubles', the length of two needles, then straightened by being packed tightly into two iron rings, heated, placed on a bench and rolled backwards and forwards with a rubbing file for twenty minutes. Originally wires were 'pointed' with a hand-operated grindstone, which, although a fairly light operation, was a lethal one for the worker. He sat in front of the spinning wheel rolling several wires in his hands to taper the ends to a long point, and could not avoid inhaling the particles of stone and steel. Pneumoconiosis, known as 'pointer's disease' or 'rot', affected them all within a couple of years and few lived beyond thirty years of age. The old pointing shops were filthy holes, yet there was no shortage of workers as a pointer earned £4 a week compared with an average of ten shillings (50p) elsewhere in the industry. In 1846 an automatic pointing machine and extractor fan were introduced, but at first the men refused to work with them and went on strike, fearing that they would lead to a reduction in wages. Heads and eyes were impressed by a man using a very heavy, kick-stamp drop-hammer which handled 30,000 doubles a day, but the next task, 'eyeing', could be done more cheaply by using two women, who had to work flat out to keep up with him. After surplus metal was removed, the eyed needles were 'spitted' (threaded on a strip of metal) by women and children as young as three years old. The needles were hardened, then tempered to restore their resilient state before being scoured. About 50,000 needles were packed into sackcloth bundles with an abrasive, soft soap and water and trundled back and forth under heavy rollers for up to eight hours, then rinsed and the entire process repeated three to seven times, depending on the quality of the finished product. They were dried in rotating barrels of hot sand or sawdust.

Needles are made in millions – in 1890 Milwards produced a million a day and by 1950 thirty-five million a week – but it is the needles that are bought and not used that boost profits. Many old packets still have some of their original contents.

1 *Lewis, Wright & Bayliss catalogue or traveller's samples, 1886,*
National Needle Museum, Redditch

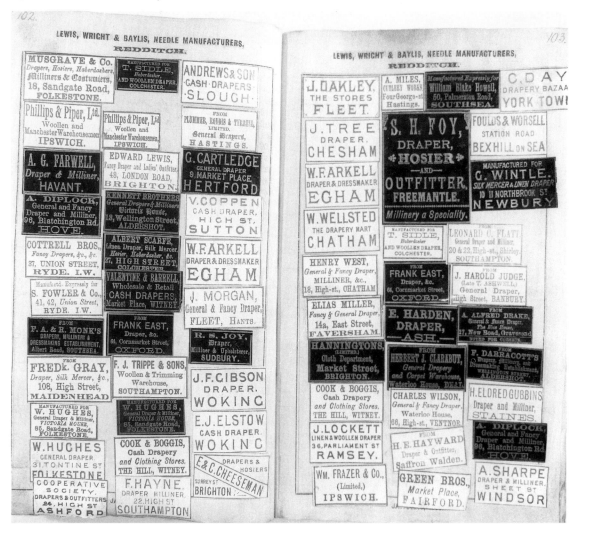

Hundreds of different packets of needles made during the past 150 years have survived, but it is impossible to list all the makers. One reason was that businesses were continually merging and, as any interference with a brand name could easily upset customers, it was in everyone's interest to perpetuate it. For example, in 1927 the Crescent Manufacturing Company, owned by the London wholesaler Olney, Amsden and Sons, joined Milwards, but 'Crescent' needles continued to be made for many years. Another problem was caused by firms that bought partly-finished or finished needles from makers and sold them under their own name. The reason shops wanted to promote their name is obvious, but it is surprising that a large company like Kirby Beard should have ceased making needles in the 1870s, bought supplies from Milwards, and packed them under their own name for more than sixty years.

The giants of the trade were Milwards (1730), Morrall (1750) and Hall (1842). Sixty other firms who were in business in 1900 eventually combined with one of these three. Milward and Hall merged in 1930 and became the Needle Industries Group Ltd, and Abel Morrall, who made Aero Needles, joined them in 1984. They are now all part of Coats Viyella PLC.

It is not possible to date needles with any accuracy, but the wrappers can be arranged in chronological order (in the trade they were 'put-up' into packets). At the beginning of the nineteenth century most needles were sold loose wrapped in dark blue, grey or black acid-free paper with the type, size and maker hand-written or printed on a white label. Trade marks were rarely used before 1840. Labels bearing the name and address of a shop were popular between 1870–1920 (fig 1). Fancy labels were used between 1860–1940, with their heyday in 1870–1930, and among a varied range of subjects they illustrated historical events, inventions, famous people and exhibitions, and were influenced by artistic styles. Although it might be possible to date them from the illustration, it must be remembered that some designs continued long after they were newsworthy. In 1886 Lewis, Wright and Bayliss claimed to have invented the 'Thyral needle with a silk-stuck wrapper' but it is unclear what this implied. It was not until about 1900 that most makers fixed needles into a small piece of cloth (waxed paper was used in the 1930s) which was known as 'pin-stuck', as this was the accepted way with pins. The small aperture to view the eyes was introduced in about 1920 and a piece of celluloid added a few years later, to be replaced by non-inflammable material in the 1940s. The most recent development was the blister pack, 1960, with the whole needle visible. The design of needle packets was influenced by a chance meeting in 1855 between J.W. Milward and G.A. Clark, the thread manufacturer, when on a journey to the USA. They became friends on the boat and shared an office in New York. Later Milward merged with the Boye Needle Company of Chicago, who had contacts with the chain stores and insisted that British makers improve their needle packets.

Some needle packets, together with other tools and accessories, can be dated from a registration mark. Patents were available from the late seventeenth century, but in the 1830s a committee recommended that a copyright system should be established in Great Britain, and the *Design Copyright Act* was passed in 1839. From 1842–83 new designs could be registered and given a diamond-shaped mark from which, with the aid of a table, the date of registration could be determined. In 1883 the *Patents, Design and Trademark Act* was passed and the diamond mark replaced by a registration number. If fully marked, the year of registration can be obtained from information held at the Public Record Office in Kew, Surrey, but unfortunately some makers used only 'Registered' without a number or 'Patent Applied For'.

George Baxter, the inventor of printing with oil-based colours, found there was strong competition to promote the sale of needles. Between 1850–59 Baxter and his licencees produced coloured prints to decorate small boxes which held a packet of needles, and his son,

2 *Baxter Prints on needle boxes, 1850–70*, Tunbridge Wells Municipal Museum and Art Gallery

3 *Avery case for needle packets, 1870–95,* Gloucester Folk Museum

George, continued to supply these until the 1870s. The needle prints were made in sheets divided into approximately 1 in × 2 in (25mm × 51mm) sections showing a dozen or so different subjects. The sets of decorated boxes fitted into a larger box which was also embellished with a print. Some uncut sheets of prints have survived, but few boxes remain and most are empty. Single prints were also put on slightly larger boxes and needle books covered in velvet or embossed paper. Other printers, especially in Germany, copied Baxter's idea, but they used inferior designs and weak colours. A few needlemakers, notably Kirby Beard, sold boxes containing their own needles, but from the small amount of evidence available it seems likely that the majority were bought by shops and wholesalers (sometimes known as factors) who also purchased the needles and packaged them under their own name: 'C. Stocken, 53 Regent Street, London' must have been a shop, and 'Josslyn's Queen Drill'd Eye Needles, London' a wholesaler. A box in Worthing Museum contains French-made needles. During the first half of the nineteenth century some very attractive boxes were made to hold packets of needles and were strong enough to be re-filled when empty instead of being discarded, unlike so many of the Baxter ones. Probably the most charming were caskets shaped like miniature Georgian knife boxes made of tortoise-shell (actually the shell of a turtle), ivory or wood, especially Tunbridge and Mauchline Ware (see Chapter 2, and colour illustrations 5, 6 and 7). Less durable were leather cases in the shape of a miniature book with a black and white print inside which were probably of German manufacture.

During the second half of the nineteenth century, probably after 1865, there was a fashion to market packets of needles in decorative metal containers made of stamped brass or bronze in realistic shapes – butterflies, shells, animals, miniature furniture, buildings and innumerable caskets. The majority of them bear the name of a Redditch needlemaker, William Avery, whose cases were well-made and clearly marked, with some designs patented. Identical shapes were, however, made with other names impressed and these

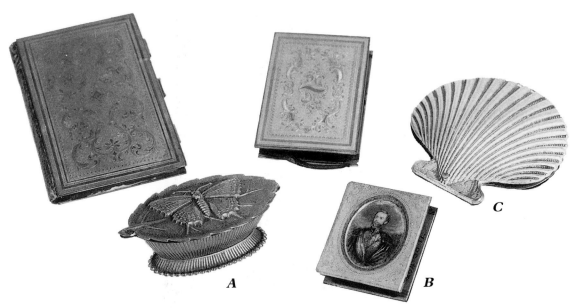

4 *Metal cases for needle packets, mid to late nineteenth century: (front, left to right) a – Avery, b – Baxter print, c – Crossley,* York Castle Museum

may have been under licence or produced to order for a special customer. The popular 'Quadruple Golden Casket', which held four packets of needles and was registered in 1868, was sometimes marked 'G. & J. Morton, Cheapside', who was probably a drapers' wholesaler in the City of London, an area much favoured until the bombing during the Second World War. Avery cases were produced in greatest numbers between 1870–95 (figs 3 and 4). Cheaper, tin-plate copies were imported from Germany until 1914.

'The Mitrailleuse' needle holder was first advertised in the 1880s. The name originated from a French breech-loading gun with several barrels. It was a metal cylinder, about 3 in (77mm) long divided into several compartments, and held about fifty needles of various sizes; by revolving the top and tilting the case, one needle of the required size emerged through a hole in the lid. Several makers patented a mitrailleuse, but there was little difference between them; the majority had the name of a needlemaker, wholesaler or department store and a few were decorated with a printed picture. Metal mitrailleuses were made until the mid-1930s when they cost $4\frac{1}{2}$d (about 2p); plastic was used from 1931 by D.F. Tayler's for 'Nita' and Milward's for 'The Serpent'. A wooden mitrailleuse for sewing machine needles was imported from Germany and a few silver examples were made in France.

Needle-cases holding a range of needles in various sizes have been made or marketed by various firms since the 1880s. The leading maker was Abel Morrall. Many were decorative and very practical,

5 *Two boxes for needles, shown open and closed,* c.*1900,*
York Castle Museum

but ladies have always sought alternative holders for their needles
(see figs 5, 6, 7a–c).

When needles were very expensive, some needlewomen kept
them on their person, hanging from the waist in a small holder. By
the seventeenth century, many ladies owned a hand-made needle
book and they have been made continuously since then, although
few pre-1800 books have survived and the majority are from much
later. The leaves were made of flannel, felt or Kerseymere, a fine
twilled woollen cloth named after the village in Suffolk where it was
woven. The popularity of bazaars and the desire to give small hand-
made gifts to a large circle of friends and relatives were responsible
for the number of needle books and other trifles that proliferated in
Victorian and Edwardian times, often made from instructions
published in contemporary journals. Sometimes suitable items for
sale were amassed in a Charity or Jew's Basket (this originated from
a Society formed in an attempt to convert Jews to Christianity and

6 *Leather case of needles, early twentieth century,*
National Needle Museum, Redditch

was mentioned by Jane Austen and Charlotte Brontë). Assorted bits
and pieces were assembled in a basket and sent to a friend who would
use some of them to make a few novelties, put them into the basket
with some of her own off-cuts and deliver it to another address.

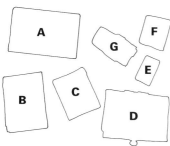

7 *Needle books.   a/b Abel Morrall, plastic covered print 1935;
print on card c.1900   c John James, raffia, c.1930   d, e, f Hand-
made plush c.1890, silk c.1870, 'MIZPAH', c.1890*
g A tartan housewife 'Made by the ladies of Winchester', 1914–18

Perforated card, or Bristol board, was used for needle books and
disc pincushions between 1820 and 1910. The board, named after
the Earl of Bristol around 1800, was a firm laminate of several sheets
of paper, punched with holes in a regular or decorative pattern
which could be embellished with beads, silks or fine wools. The
earliest examples showed a preference for long stitches in silk, but
after 1840 cross stitch and beadwork were influenced by Berlin
Wool Work, and religious mottoes date from 1850 onwards. Some
card imported from Germany during the second half of the century
had embossed borders and later printed details (fig 8).

The use of perforated card was an amateur pastime. Straw work,
although also hand-work, was not attempted by ladies at home. It
was made from split straw, sometimes dyed, and woven into a

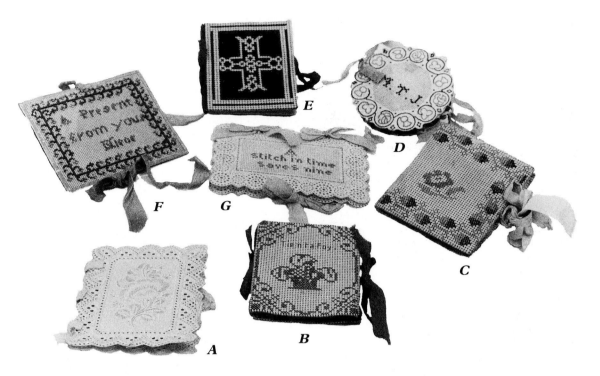

8 *Needle books of card, 1840–80. a Embossed and punched
b, c Silk – perforated   d Silk – perforated and punched
e Wool – perforated f Beads and wool – perforated   g Silk –
perforated and punched,* York Castle Museum

pattern. It was fashionable from the 1750s to the 1820s and may have
reached Britain from France via prisoners-of-war who brought the
skill with them. Between 1797 and 1814 prisoners at Norman Cross
Barracks, Peterborough, collected and dried 'grasses' for this work
and obtained different shades by steeping them in tea.

Small, decorative containers to hold a few needles in a work box
were made from about 1790 and throughout the following century.
There were two basic shapes – slim and rectangular mother-of-
pearl, or cylindrical in silver, silver-gilt, ivory, bone, tortoise-shell,
wood or other materials. All had tight-fitting lids and were
decorated in various ways. Until 1840 most cases were very fine, but
there was an ever-increasing demand for work box accessories and
quality gave way to quantity. Some features may help to date the
earlier needle-cases. An inner lining of tortoise-shell was usually
replaced by one of bone after 1810 and any case of tortoise-shell was
unusual after 1840. Steel studding was fashionable until the 1830s.
The early carved ivories, including the charming pea-pods, cannot
be compared with later examples in bone. Ivory does not always
imply elephant ivory, however; examples may be made of walrus

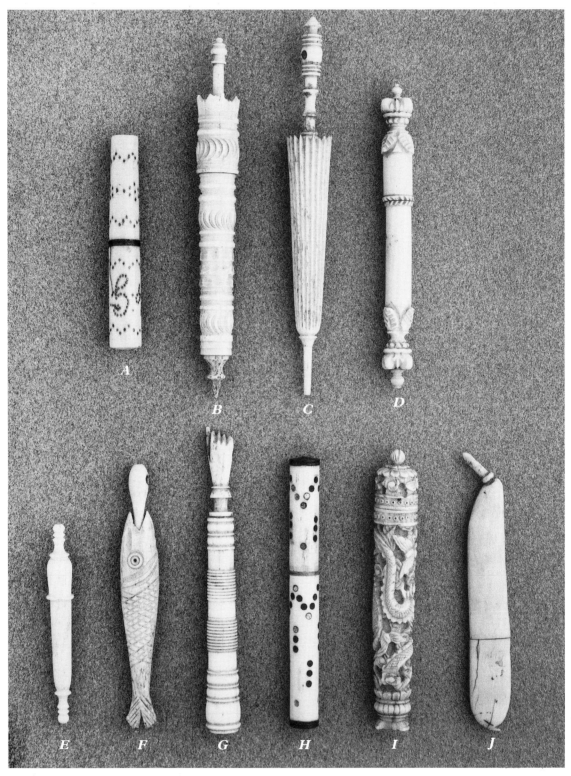

9 *Needlecases from c.1840.   a, h Piqué (steel studs) on ivory,*
1840   b, e Bone   c, f, g Bone with Stanhope, 1860+   d Ivory e
Bone   i Chinese ivory, 1850   j Ivory (Walrus?)

tusk, which was sometimes carved by sailors and known as scrimshaw. Many of the finest early needlecases were imported from France, including those made of bone and covered with minute beads, threaded on fine wire to form a spiral or dot pattern [colour illustration 2].

Souvenirs were made to suit all tastes but they were not all of practical value and many were destined for the display cabinet rather than the work box. Among such novelties were Stanhopes, small trifles, usually bone but occasionally of wood, with a little peep-hole that contained a lens which magnified twenty-five times and which, when held very close to the eye, revealed with exceptional clarity a topological view or verse. They were invented by the Earl of Stanhope in 1850 and production began in France in 1860 (figs 9c, f and g). Today they are made in Hong Kong from plastic. The British souvenir industry expanded after 1840 with the development of the railways. Souvenirs from other European countries, Egypt and the Holy Land were unusual until Thomas Cook's tours, the first of which was in 1841, but remained uncommon until after 1875.

Some decorative cases are too large for sewing needles and may have been used for small netting or crochet tools or bodkins. It is difficult to be precise, but most cases of this size are from the nineteenth century. The only difference between a bodkin and a needle is size, although some bodkins made for threading ribbons were flat and others may terminate in a knob. Until the end of the seventeenth century men and women needed long bodkins, 7 in (12cm) or more in length, for rethreading the fastenings on their clothing. In the following century they became shorter but were still hand-made and thick in section compared with later tools. Bodkins of silver engraved with initials, a date, or a few words were popular after 1750 (fig 10n).

Although bone bodkins with simple or no decoration continued to be made, after needle mills introduced machinery metal bodkins were mass-produced by all the large needlemakers. A few were stamped with commemorations of royal or other events in the first half of the nineteenth century and later with political slogans, maybe to influence men through their wives (figs 10h and l). The bodkin acquired a new use when elastic was invented in 1840.

After 1900 bodkins were sold with fancy names on cards: 'The Slip-Thro Ribbon Threader' or 'The Patent Holdfast'. Milwards were still supplying bone bodkins in 1931, but since 1945 all bodkins have been made of cheap metal or plastic.

The problem of threading a fine needle had concerned inventors since the early nineteenth century, and one of the first solutions was a needle with a calyx eye. Milwards immediately bought the rights to produce it, but probably did not market the idea until the 1850s. The eye had two compartments and terminated in a V-shaped notch: 'It can be threaded immediately by looping the thread over the head of the needle and drawing downward through the slot into the first eye

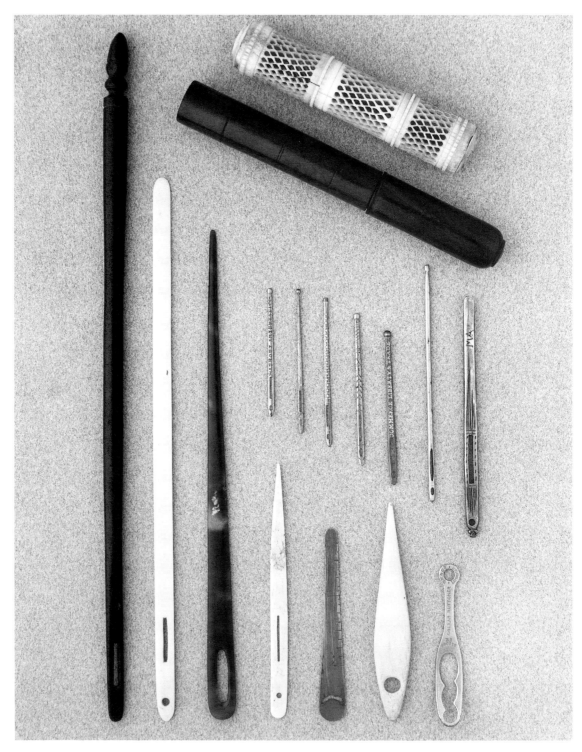

10 *Bodkins.   Ribbon threaders: a wood,
eighteenth century;   b bone, nineteenth
century;   c tortoise-shell, 1840;   d bone;
e Elastic threader, 1920   f Bone cord threader,
nineteenth century   g Collar buttoner, 1930*

*h–l Bodkins with slogans, 1880–1920   m Gilt,
nineteenth century   n Silver, seventeenth century
o Wooden case, early nineteenth century
p Prisoner-of-war work? c.1810*

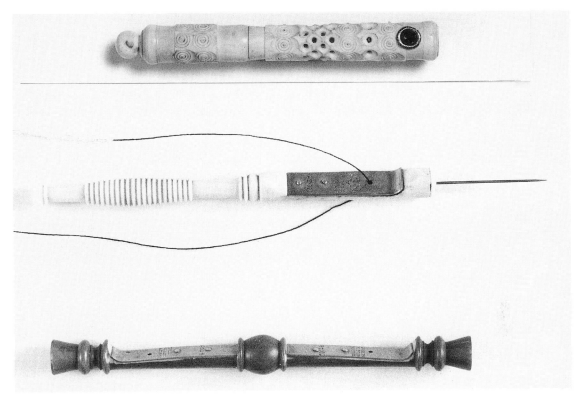

11 *Nineteenth-century needle threaders*, City of Salford Museums
and Art Galleries

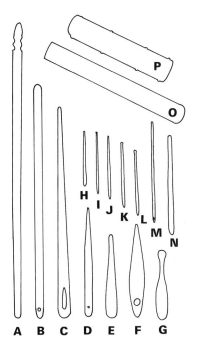

and then into the second eye. The thread cannot pull out again'. Kirby Beard made 'The Society Self-Threading Needle' which had a delicate latchet hook in the eye which was sprung open with the thread, and in 1867 patented the 'Scientific Needle – the eye when threaded only equals the size of the body of the needle'.

The first accessory made to help thread a needle may have been a device shown at The Great Exhibition of 1851 by Joseph Rogers of Sheffield. It was made of ivory: 'The top portion above the handle is flat on which a small metal plate is fixed through which a small hole is pierced, a corresponding hole being in the ivory of larger size. The needle is passed through it, the eye fitting exactly over that in the plate so the thread passes through the three holes at once'. Several other makers produced similar devices in bone and wood during the second half of the nineteenth century (fig 11). After 1900 more ingenious ideas were devised, but some instructions are difficult to understand. Eventually, a simple wire on a small metal or card holder replaced all the other types and was extremely effective (fig 12).

12 *Twentieth-century needle threaders*, City of Salford Museums and Art Galleries

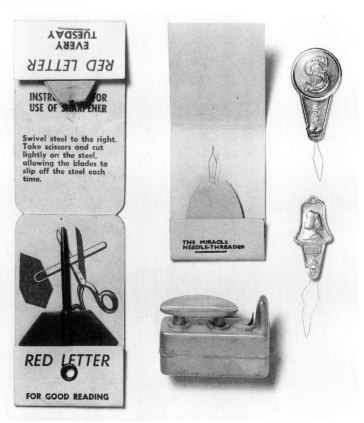

CHAPTER 2
Threads

The earliest yarns were spun with a distaff and spindle weighted with a whorl. The first crude spinning wheel was invented in the mid-1500s, but the familiar flying spinning wheel was not used until the eighteenth century, when several machines were developed which followed the principles from which modern techniques evolved for mass production.

13 *Linen threads made c.1900*, Lisburn Museum, Co. Antrim

Flax is the stem fibre of *linium usitatissium* and is used to make linen. Wild flax grown in Britain was spun from the first century AD but fine thread was not available until it was manufactured in Scotland and Ireland during the eighteenth century. In 1784 John Barbour from Paisley, Scotland, established his first mill in Ireland near Lisburn, County Antrim. It became the Linen Thread Company in 1898 when Barbour mills in Ireland, New Jersey and New York, USA, merged with Finlayson, Bousfield of Scotland and Massachusetts, USA, and W. & K. Knox of Scotland, making it one of the world's largest producers of linen thread. In the drapery trade 'thread' always implied linen thread. Among brands in a 1905 catalogue were Barbour, Knox and Finlayson, but the name Finlayson had disappeared by 1930 and today all the threads are marketed under the Barbour label by the Hanson Trust. At one time a few other mills produced domestic threads but most of their output was for commercial use. Some packaging of linen threads was attractive, notably boxes containing skeins (fig 13).

Silk probably originated in China and was imported into Britain from medieval times. By the seventeenth century raw silk also came from India and Italy, but was very expensive. An attempt was made to develop a home industry by planting mulberry trees, on which the silk moth caterpillar feeds, but unfortunately black mulberry was chosen instead of white and the experiment failed, although some of the trees still remain in large gardens. Silk for domestic use has always been sold in skeins without fancy packaging, but sometimes these were ingeniously wound to prevent tangling.

During the eighteenth century Paisley became an important centre for silk weaving. From the 1790s Peter and James Clark worked there making heddles for looms, but in 1806 disaster struck the whole industry, as a result of the Berlin Decree of Napoleon, which declared that France would go to war with any country which traded with Britain. Although some silk was smuggled into the country, the Paisley industry declined and Peter Clark began to experiment making heddles for cotton, which proved to be very successful. In 1812 the Clark family of Anchor Mills claimed to be the first commercial producers of sewing cotton in Great Britain.

Cotton textiles had been known in Britain since the thirteenth century. Some raw cotton was imported by the East India Companies at the beginning of the seventeenth century followed by larger quantities from North America after 1780, but there were few machines capable of spinning good quality sewing cotton and needlewomen still preferred linen. As Mrs Delany wrote in 1766, 'cotton is not strong enough to bear the working'.

Soon after Clark had established his mill, many more were re-opened and at the peak there were over a hundred firms in Paisley producing cotton yarn. One was James Coats, who started a small mill in 1826, and by 1846 three-quarters of his production was exported to the United States. During 1864, in an effort to boost his

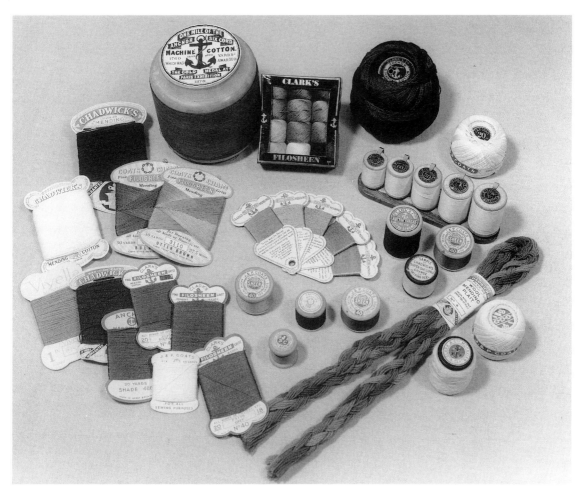

14 *Sewing and crochet cotton with various mending threads,*
1900–40, J. & P. Coats Ltd

sales to the USA, Clark built a mill at Newark, New Jersey, but, not
to be outdone, Coats opened one at Pawtucket, Rhode Island, in
1870. There was great rivalry between the two companies, both in
Scotland and America, but in 1896 they amalgamated under the
Coats name and were joined by James Chadwick of Bolton,
Lancashire. All three names continued to appear on yarns for some
years but eventually Chadwick was dropped. Now, as part of Coats
Viyella PLC, it is one of the largest thread producers in the world.

Raw cotton consists of fibres or staples which should be of a
minimum length of one and a quarter inches (31mm) for good
quality sewing thread, as short staples make it weak. Cotton fibre is
converted into finished thread by carding, which disentangles and
removes some short strands, then it is combed to remove the

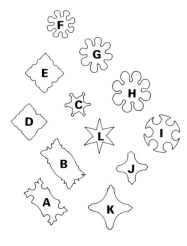

15 *Thread winders, nineteenth century.* *a, b, c Bone*
d, e Blue and green glass, 1880 f, k Mother-of-pearl
g Tortoise-shell h Ivory i Horn j Jet l Silver

remaining short fibres, which are not wasted but spun into cheaper threads. Several combed slivers are drawn out and combined into one sliver which is drawn out still further, given a slight twist, and becomes a rove or roving. *The Workwoman's Guide*, 1835, suggested that if a fine cotton was required, rovings from a thicker one could be used. Cotton is spun into a single yarn of the required thickness and twisted to form the appropriate ply of thread required. Nowadays, once a yarn has been twisted it is called 'thread' but previously 'twist' was common at the drapers and it is still used on some labels. In 1835 John Mercer discovered that thread treated with caustic soda had added strength, lustre and more absorbent qualities. Mercerised thread was soon in production and, as it did not require waxing before use, the decorative waxer went out of fashion.

To manufacture linen thread the flax is first retted (soaked) to facilitate the separation of the fibres from the woody tissue by beating. Subsequently it is treated similarly to cotton.

Although cotton threads were made elsewhere, it was in Paisley that the system of numbering was settled in the early years. Most threads are three-cord or six-cord. Three-cord yarn was named according to the count of a single yarn: 30's three-cord is made from three strands of 30's single cotton – 30's single cotton is 30 hanks, each of 840 yards, weighing one pound. With six-cord cotton, the thread numbers are retained but a single yarn twice as fine is used; 30's six-cord is made from six strands of 60's single cotton. The finished thread is the same thickness whether three or six-cord. The thickness or gauge of a thread is indicated by numbers and in the past a very large range of sizes was available suitable for coarse calico or the finest nainsook. In 1890 one manufacturer produced eighteen increments between Nos. 10–200.

There were various experiments to produce man-made fibre. Credit is given to a Frenchman, Hilare de Chardonnet, who made a chemical fibre from cellulose in 1884, but it was not a commercial success. A great breakthrough came when viscose was developed. It was patented in Britain in 1892 and production began in 1905. The yarn was called artificial silk until 1924, when the name was changed to rayon. Until the late 1930s there were only two man-made fibres, rayon and acetate (Celanese), both derived from trees or cotton. A truly man-made fibre was discovered by the Du Pont Company, Delaware, USA, in 1930 and the production of nylon began in 1938. An acrylic fibre, Orlon, was introduced in 1951 and polyester, invented in 1941, was manufactured as Terylene in 1955. Today there are many names for the various man-made fibres. Some are made into threads as they are, others are blended with natural fibres.

Small amounts of thread, especially silk, were stored on thread

16 *Wooden thread winders, nineteenth century.   a, b Oak,*
rosewood   c Souvenir 1863   d Straw   e, h Tunbridge Ware
f, i Swiss   g Rosewood, 1810

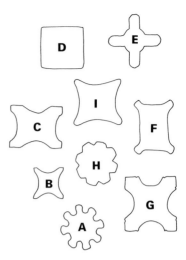

winders, the simplest being a tiny roll of soft paper. It was the
practice in some shops to sell a few strands of coloured silk from a
larger, cut skein and wind them on a scrap of paper before wrapping
them up. Purpose-made thread winders have been made over a long
period, and they are not easy to date. They can be made from any
smooth material – ivory, bone, wood, mother-of-pearl, tortoise-
shell, metal, glass, horn or fancy card and decorated in a variety of
ways (figs 15 and 16). Horn was very cheap and plentiful and was
usually ground up, heated and pressed into moulds. Most eighteenth-century winders were fine quality and delicate. Any winder
with carved or painted initials and a date may have been a love token.
Large quantities of pretty winders were imported and made in
Britain between 1800–40, but during the second half of the century,
especially after 1880, some winders were more practical than
decorative. Large, cross-shaped pieces of wood, either plain or
painted in pastel colours, were popular in the 1920s and 1930s and
plastic winders can still be bought today. Whether plain or
decorated, winders must hold the thread securely, usually by means
of prominent indentations, but sometimes by less obvious methods;
for example the winder of straw (fig 16d) has no means of holding the
thread firmly and the two glass winders (figs 15d and e) could easily
be overlooked. The souvenir from Herne's Oak (fig 16c) is rare. In
1863 an autumn gale brought down this tree which was reputed to
have stood in Home Park, Windsor, for 620 years. According to
tradition, a Royal keeper of that name had turned poacher and
hanged himself from it in remorse. Shakespeare referred to it as
haunted in *The Merry Wives of Windsor*.

Occasionally small, fish-shapes of bone, ivory or mother-of-pearl
are found empty or with some thread wound around the tail end.
The Department of Textiles, Furnishing and Dress at the Victoria
and Albert Museum and the Textile Department at Sotheby's are
both fairly certain these were made as gaming counters and not for
needlework. However, they agree they were useful objects, found in
many homes, especially in the combined games/work tables of the
late eighteenth and early nineteenth centuries, and some were
certainly used to hold thread.

Multiple winders on a rod of bone or ivory (fig 17a) were fitted
into work boxes between 1790 and 1830. Flat, multiple winders
were made throughout the nineteenth century and are still available
today, although most 'tortoiseshell' examples are plastic.

Diderot's *Dictionnaire des Sciences*, 1763, illustrated skeins of silk,
balls of linen thread and spools of metal thread. The terms spool,
reel or bobbin are regional and in some circumstances interchange-

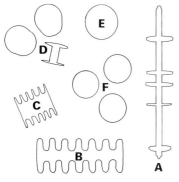

17 *Multiple spools and reels for thread.   a Multiple spool of bone from a work box, 1790–1820   b Multiple spool of tortoiseshell celluloid, 1890–1930   c Multiple spool in Tartan ware, mid nineteenth century   d Bone reels from a work box, 1820   e Asian reel holder of bone with end-grain mosaic of metal, ebony, shell, etc., from a work box, 1820–50   f French? reel holders of mother-of-pearl and bone from mid nineteenth-century work boxes*

able. The silks are shown in plaits or wrapped in paper, but during the nineteenth century some were sold in the form of a tassel, with one end of the thread wound tightly around the skein for half to three-quarters of its length. It is not known when thread was first sold in balls, but in the Victoria and Albert Museum a small box for threads with separate compartments, each with a bone eyelet, is dated as eighteenth century. There is no doubt that balls were well-established by 1813, when a travelling compendium (in the same museum) was given to Princess Charlotte, daughter of the Prince Regent. It contains a dated loyal address and among the fittings are eight compartments, six of which have their original, unused, fine linen thread balls in numbered sizes.

Individual bone, and a few ivory, spools were made from the late eighteenth century until the 1830s. Large, plain reels were probably used in workrooms and the smaller, decorated examples, sometimes with a little screw knob to hold the end of the thread, were for domestic use. Some reels had a maker's label attached to the shank, not the end, which may indicate they were returned to be refilled.

A charming and practical accessory for small quantities of thread was known as a cotton barrel, but it could also easily hold silk. None are likely to be pre-1800 as the majority came from fitted work boxes that favoured single or multiple winders in the eighteenth century, and few were made after 1835 as they were superseded by non-returnable wooden reels. They were all small and the majority made from ivory or bone, although a few were wood. The thread was wound on a small spindle which protruded through a screw-on lid and emerged through a small hole in the side, some barrels had a cranked handle to make rewinding easier. The spindle may have been returned to a shop for rewinding but there is insufficient evidence of this to be conclusive.

Some tools and accessories, including cotton barrels, were of Asian origin and incorrectly made: the beehive, fig 18d, has no hole in the eyelet and the barrel, fig 18c, no spindle. It is assumed that merchants sent examples of various needlework tools that had been made in Britain or France to India and China to be copied, to take advantage of cheap materials and labour, but that the local craftsmen failed to understand their function. However, some oriental work was superb. A fitted box of wood inlaid with ivory at York Castle Museum, c.1860 (colour picture 3) contains beautiful tools and also provides a fascinating glimpse of its nineteenth-century owner. Among an assortment of oddments in the lower compartment is a list of boy's clothing, a prescription for some medication and the husband's account book for household expenses – the sweet smell of cedarwood, a natural moth deterrent, is very strong.

Needlework boxes gradually evolved during the eighteenth century for the wealthier families but before 1780 they were very expensive and not common until after 1800. However, from the

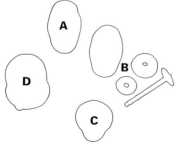

18 *Cotton barrels. a, b Early nineteenth-century ivory*
c Asian ivory without a spindle, 1830   d Vegetable ivory beehive
without a hole in the eyelet, 1840

1850s to the early years of the twentieth century, boxes for sewing
tools were varied, plentiful and often cheap. The majority were sold
with a selection of tools and accessories, while others were
purchased empty and fitted out to order at shops specializing in
fancy goods – a rosewood box, *c.*1860, in the Victoria and Albert
Museum, has matching bone reel, emery and wax holders with '1/-'
(one shilling/5p) written underneath each item. Most boxes had

scissors, thimble, bodkin and a stiletto, to which could be added holders for thread, a needle case and almost anything else for plain sewing or a variety of crafts. Some boxes can be dated approximately by the choice of tools they contain – for example cotton barrels would pre-date reel holders – but very few boxes have a complete set of fittings and some of them may be replacements. If the lining of silk or paper has a pattern, it may be possible to compare this with other fabrics of known age, but most boxes have a plain lining. Although there were fashions in colours, the staff concerned with upholstery at the Victoria and Albert Museum are reluctant to date plain fabrics.

The date of the introduction of non-returnable wooden reels is not known, but details about James Clark are interesting. When he began making sewing cotton in 1812 it was sold in skeins, but before long he offered to wind the thread on to a wooden reel for an extra halfpenny, which was refunded on return. (The reels were made from trees on the Isle of Arran until it was denuded.) This practice lasted for a very short time and by 1820 all Clark's sewing cottons were sold ready-wound on non-returnable reels. It is reasonable to suppose that other mills soon copied the idea and hundreds of makers produced an enormous range of wooden reels, cards, skeins, balls and novelty containers for sewing thread, until the introduction of the plastic reel in 1966. Some of the labels bore the name of a town, but these must be regarded with caution. One Leicester mill produced an attractive reel with a design of a shopper at a drapery counter and the motto, 'Industry Promotes Wealth' pressed into one end, and another c.1830 had reels impressed with a coat of arms, but Leicester Museum believes all threads made in the town were for the local stocking industry, not for domestic use. Around the turn of the century a deceitful practice was perpetrated by some threadmakers, who used a barrel-shaped reel which appeared to hold more than it did. Mile and half-mile reels of cotton were made from the 1890s–1930s. During the 1939–45 war manufacturers were forced to economize and some thread was sold on card spools with no end papers.

Although wooden reels were practical, they were not elegant and so decorative holders for them were made between 1830–70 (figs 17e and f). Reel holders had an ornamental top made of ivory, bone, mother-of-pearl or wood (especially Tunbridge Ware), with a slim shank and usually a plain base. The parts either screwed together or had a long pin attached to the top which slotted into the hollow shank fixed to the base. Unfortunately, when sets of reel holders were in their compartments in a work box only the fancy tops were visible and the colours of the threads were hidden. Reel holders cannot be dated accurately by size, material or design. Comparisons were made between several dated work boxes, with complete sets of reel holders, from the collection made by Queen Mary and now in the Victoria and Albert Museum. An early nineteenth-century box has five medium-sized, plain bone holders; and ebony box, *c.*1850, contains seven large holders with exceptionally thick pearl ends; a papier mâché example made by Jennings and Betteridge, *c.*1860, has six large, very plain pearl holders and a rosewood example, dated 1870, has bone holders almost identical in design to those in the earliest box.

Busy needlewomen, maybe professional dressmakers or milliners, kept reels of thread on pegs fixed to a simple wooden board (fig 14). Every shop of any size had a workroom where garments were made to measure and buckram, straw or felt hat shapes were trimmed to order; a large shop would have a special department for bonnet trimmings. For the lady at home there were decorative holders called reel or bobbin stands which could be displayed in the drawing room or parlour. The earliest stands were made about 1840 from polished wood with four or six wooden pegs and perhaps a velvet pincushion on top. After 1850 they became taller and more ornate, but as the years passed many were so elaborate and such terrible dust-traps that they were no longer practical; some were reduced to mere ornaments kept under a glass shade, while others must have been relegated to the attic, which probably accounts for the poor condition of many of them today. York Castle Museum has a collection of bobbin stands, including a very attractive one in the window of the haberdashers in the Victorian street. In store, there are a few small wooden stands and some large, very ugly, late nineteenth-century examples; one particularly useless object, made from a slice of a tree trunk, is very heavy and yet has only five pegs for reels; other stands of metal have intricate tiers of spindles to hold much larger quantities of thread. After 1900 they went out of fashion although a few were made from bakelite plastic, (colour illustration 12p), but recently new wooden ones have appeared in craft shops.

The British wooden souvenir industry had two important centres, Tunbridge Wells in Kent and Mauchline in Ayrshire, Scotland. Needlework tools and accessories featured prominently among their wares and included thread winders, thread boxes, pin discs, pincushions, sewing and knitting needle cases, knitting wool holders, tatting shuttles, darning blocks and boxes for scissors, measures, waxers and thimbles.

Tunbridge Wells had had a thriving local industry making souvenirs since visitors first came to take the waters in the mid seventeenth century, but few needlework tools were made before 1790. During the whole of the nineteenth century, output was prolific and widely marketed, but after 1900 it began to decline and production ceased in 1939. The various styles are illustrated in colour illustration 5.

In the early nineteenth century plain wood was decorated with painted coloured bands – usually red and black or green and yellow. Among the wares were needlework clamps and holders for thread, measures and thimbles. Some were further embellished with a small label – 'Remember the Giver', 'A Token of Friendship', 'A Trifle from Bath' or 'A Present from Worthing'. Less frequently, polychrome floral patterns were hand-painted or the wood was carved and painted into delightful tiny thatched cottages or turretted castles, no more than an inch (25mm) high, with a thimble or tape measure inside.

Cube and vandyke patterns, created from natural coloured woods, were made throughout the nineteenth century and probably continued into the 1920s. They are difficult to date, but after 1840 some had fancy bandings. This style of decoration was only suitable for flat objects such as needle books.

Stick Ware, carved from solid, laminated blocks of wood, and Half-Square Mosaic, cut as slices from these blocks, were made between 1820–1930, but neither can be dated accurately. Stick Ware was popular for novelties – acorn-shaped thimble holders or miniature teapot pin-cushions; Half-Square Mosaic was used for the ends of reel holders, waxers, measures or thread winders and was less common after 1900.

End-grain Mosaic is often called Tunbridge Ware. The design was made from various natural-coloured woods which gave the appearance of a true mosaic and was first produced in the late 1820s, coinciding with the popularity of Berlin Wool Work. For this embroidery the design was drawn on graph paper and coloured, then copied square by square on to canvas using wool or silk; some Tunbridge Ware mosaics used Berlin patterns, but most were created especially. Although no one would deny end-grain mosaic was the work of craftsmen, it is deceptive and was produced with a certain amount of mass-production. Very basically it can be compared to a Battenburg cake, the pink and white cake representing two different woods, which can be cut into a large number of identical slices. Over 100 different woods were used, without any artificial staining, and a skilled man could cut thirteen slices per inch (25mm) which were then mounted on a carcass. By 1902 there was only one maker in the town; in 1926 he moved to Rye, Sussex, and struggled on until the outbreak of war.

Towards the end of the eighteenth century the souvenir industry of Scotland expanded in several towns, but needlework tools did not figure prominently until the 1830s, when William and Andrew Smith of Mauchline became the leading manufacturer, a position they would hold until 1933. All Scottish souvenir ware can be called Mauchline Ware, although most novelties were made in at least two, and possibly four, decorative finishes.

In the 1840s the Smiths invented a means of painting tartan patterns directly on wooden objects and in 1853 a machine speeded up the process by painting the pattern on to paper which was then stuck on the wood. Tartan Ware, as it is now called, was very popular and made by Smiths and other firms into the twentieth century, but on later pieces the quality is inferior and joins in the paper are visible (colour picture 6).

By 1850 the Smiths had developed another technique using transfers which were produced in very large quantities from 1860–1900 and continued to be made until the works closed in 1933. This technique is known as Mauchline Ware (colour illustration 7). Transfers of engravings were applied to light-coloured sycamore wood and finished with a thick coat of varnish. Subjects included almost every well-known place in Scotland, hundreds of views of towns, churches, castles, monuments and bridges in the rest of Britain and a considerable number of locations in France, Belgium, Spain, South Africa, Canada, Australia and the United States. Very few can be dated accurately because, although new transfers were continually added to the range, there is no evidence that the old ones were ever abandoned. The darning block (fig 70d) was purchased in the 1890s, yet the two figures are wearing clothes fashionable twenty years earlier. Most transfer plates were pre-1880, with very few made after 1890. Between 1860 and the early 1900s, some makers stuck a photograph or print on the wood as an alternative to a transfer. At about the same time, possibly 1870, a leading maker of Tunbridge Ware, Thomas Barton, introduced Decalcomanie Ware in which a polychrome design was printed on tissue paper and glued to the wood.

Also in 1870, and at Tunbridge Wells, wooden articles were advertised for fern printing and simultaneously Fern Ware was introduced in Scotland. Real ferns were used as a stencil and splattered with a thick brown pigment; fern-printed paper was substituted after 1900. Fern Ware in full colour was a transfer (colour illustration 7).

After 1860 there was a fashion for black lacquered wares decorated with a photograph or a print, often embellished with a few words or a verse.

Various boxes produced by the Mauchline industry were used by thread manufacturers to promote sales. J. & P. Coats bought their first consignment in 1866 and used these attractive containers until 1914. The name of the thread maker was always printed on a label and fixed inside the lid or on the base. The names of Coats and Clark predominate but Chadwick, Glenfield, Kerr and Medlock also used the idea. The boxes contained sewing thread, embroidery skeins, or knitting or crochet cotton. Some had compartments or pegs which could be refilled, while others made receptacles for handkerchiefs or trinkets when empty. The most amusing boxes doubled as party games with random questions and answers on the theme of love, chosen by spinning a pointer, rolling a die or revolving small knobs (colour illustration 8i).

CHAPTER 3

Scissors

Scissors of the larger sort, made like the rest with pivoted blades and handles, are sometimes called shears and may be confused with spring shears, which have neither pivots nor handles. Spring shears were used in Roman Britain and by medieval times had been adopted as the sign of a professional embroiderer. They are less complicated to manufacture than pivoted scissors, but are nonetheless a very effective tool and still made today. It is not easy to distinguish domestic shears from the tool of a craftsman in the textile industry, but those with decoration, or in a fine quality sheath, were probably used in a home.

Scissors consist of three parts: the blades, the bows (handles) and the shanks.

Scissors similar to modern pairs were also used by the Romans and although they were sometimes described as iron, steel was known and the blades at least were probably strengthened with it. Until the thirteenth century very few people in Britain owned scissors. Some were imported from France, and during the following century a few cutlers were established in Sheffield but their scissors were unsuitable for fine work. Two hundred years later, when cut-work embroidery was fashionable, those that could afford them still wanted French scissors.

During the seventeenth century, Britain began to manufacture steel suitable for good scissors, but it was very expensive and a quality product was not available at a reasonable price until crucible steel was discovered in 1700. In 1771 Robert Hinchcliffe of Sheffield was the first maker to use the new steel and other firms soon followed, but the quantities they produced were not great compared with the output in the nineteenth century. The scissors were made with the blades 'nailed' (rivetted) together, not screwed (examples of French scissors illustrated in Diderot's *Dictionnaire des Sciences*, 1763, appear to use both methods). Some British-made scissors with silver bows and shanks were extremely fine and beautiful. Early steel pairs were either left dull or polished, but the really bright, mirror-finish came later with better abrasive materials. Very few eighteenth-century scissors have survived except a few with folding handles from étuis (fig 19c). Most folding scissors were made later, including those made for nineteenth-century chatelaines (colour illustration 9).

19 *Scissors and shears. a German hot-forged with leather sheath, souvenir of marriage of the Princess Royal with Frederick III, 1858. A similar pair was made for the marriage of the Prince of Wales in 1863 b Cold-forged, c.1900 c Folding scissors from eighteenth-century étui d Shagreen case with silver mounts, late eighteenth century e Folding scissors, second half nineteenth century f Seam knife or cutter for buttonholes, nineteenth century g Shears with brass spring, late eighteenth or early nineteenth century h Steel shears i Chinese-type embroidery scissors, nineteenth century j Persian-type scissors, probably Sheffield-made, nineteenth century*

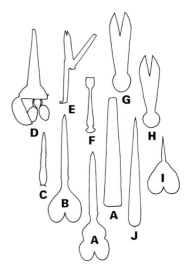

The étui was a small, decorative box for sewing and other useful implements, usually made of good quality and often expensive materials, including French enamel and even gold. They were manufactured during the eighteenth and early nineteenth centuries, but after 1800 flat sewing cases were often preferred. These included examples made in Paris with mother-of-pearl fittings (fig 25) and some silver or silver-gilt tools fitted into ivory cases made in Dieppe. These ivory cases, and some of tortoiseshell, were copied in celluloid plastic between 1880–1910. The sewing case, which made such an acceptable present, has never gone out of fashion and large numbers of leather-covered boxes, with silver or steel tools, were made throughout the nineteenth century. From the 1880s to recent times inexpensive sets were sold in department stores. Most sewing cases contained a pair of scissors, but they did not necessarily match the other contents. The 'Lady's Companion' case of sewing and other useful tools was a mid-nineteenth century adaptation of the étui, either as a box or in the form of a leather-covered book. Several variations are shown in fig 72. In the 1880s and 1890s some French sewing cases were made in the form of a handbag or miniature trunk, complete with a carrying handle and often covered in velvet with ivory or bone decorations. A leather sewing case in Worthing Museum appears to be unused, so the contents are probably original. It shows clearly the difficulty of dating some tools and accessories. There are six sets of steel knitting needles with blue stripes, which were first manufactured in the 1890s, but each of the six packets of needles, with matching labels, has a celluloid window, not used until after 1920. The case also contains two buttonhooks, a stiletto, a bodkin, a penknife, two pairs of plain scissors and an unusual item, a leather-covered book (matching the needlecase) labelled *PLAISTER*, an obsolete spelling of plaster. Occasionally a small embroidered holder for 'court plaster' was kept in the work box as first aid for a pricked finger. Another sewing case in Tudor House Museum, Southampton, is covered in red plush and this also appears to have its original contents of silver(?) thimble and needlecase, together with a stiletto, crochet hook, buttonhook and penknife with carved mother-of-pearl handles but no scissors.

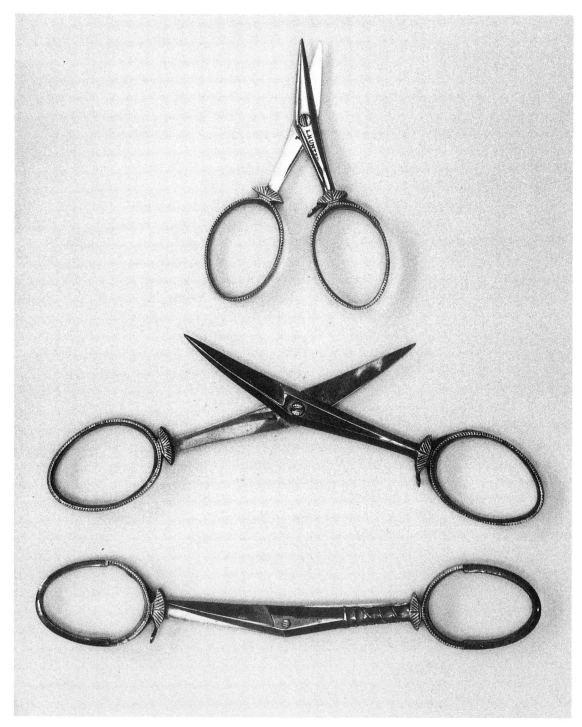

20 *Folding hand-forged scissors*, c.*1850*, Sheffield City Museums

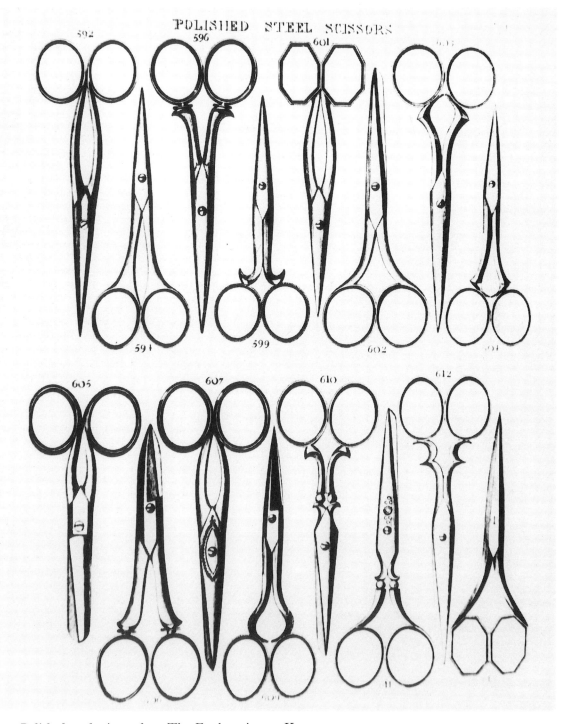

21 *Polished steel scissors from* The Explanation or Key to
the Various Manufactures of Sheffield, *Joseph Smith 1816.*
Reprinted by Early American Industries Association

Plush velvet made of silk was known by at least the sixteenth century, but during the nineteenth century the plush used on sewing cases was probably made from cotton or a silk/cotton mixture. It was very popular for these and for thimble cases towards the end of the century, but this sewing set was probably made earlier.

The medieval chatelaine was a useful accessory, having scissors, keys and other items suspended on cords or chains from a hook at the waist. By the early eighteenth century they were made of gold, silver-gilt or silver and only worn for decoration, and with the advent of slim, Empire-line dresses in the 1790s they went out of fashion. About 1840 they were re-introduced, now made of good quality steel, but from 1880 to their demise at the turn of the century, they became very ornate and of poor quality with little practical use. Very few surving étuis or chatelaines have their original fittings (colour illustration 9).

The polished steel scissors illustrated in *The Explanation or Key to the Various Manufactures of Sheffield* by Joseph Smith, 1816, (fig 21), show the elegant and restrained decoration of the period restricted to engraved motifs on plain shapes. Several of these patterns continued in production for many years and were still made when *Taylor's Eye Witness Sewing Scissor Catalogue* was printed in the 1930s. When scissors are hand-made from identical steel it is very difficult to differentiate between a nineteenth and early twentieth-century product.

By 1835 the shape of the shanks, and to a lesser extent the bows, had become very decorative. In 1851 Sheffield was producing thousands of scissors each week in a vast range of designs. It was estimated there were 120 manufacturers and no establishment had less than 2000 patterns; for example, Mr. G. Wilkinson had 7000 and Messrs Hobson betwen 5000 and 6000. The designs were known as 'filed patterns' and recorded in pattern books by craftsmen, who gave them quaint and peculiar names. There are two pattern books in the Sheffield City Museum, the majority of the designs in which have been rubbed from actual scissors using candle soot. One book has 415 different examples, each numbered and priced per dozen between three shillings and sixpence and seven shillings (about 36p) for the man's time.

The value of the raw material, steel, was a very small part of the cost compared to the labour. In 1850 a forger earned 16s – 28s, a filer 18s – 30s and a grinder 25s – 40s (£2) per week for their part in making up to twenty-four dozen pairs of scissors. The difference in the amount earned was because of payment by piecework.

The manufacturing process was described in *The Art Journal*, 1851. Scissors were forged from straight rods of steel without models or dies and relied entirely on the skill of the craftsman. Blades of identical hardness were paired, marked, and bored for a screw which gave a better adjustment than nailing. The two halves were kept together through all subsequent processes, for unless the

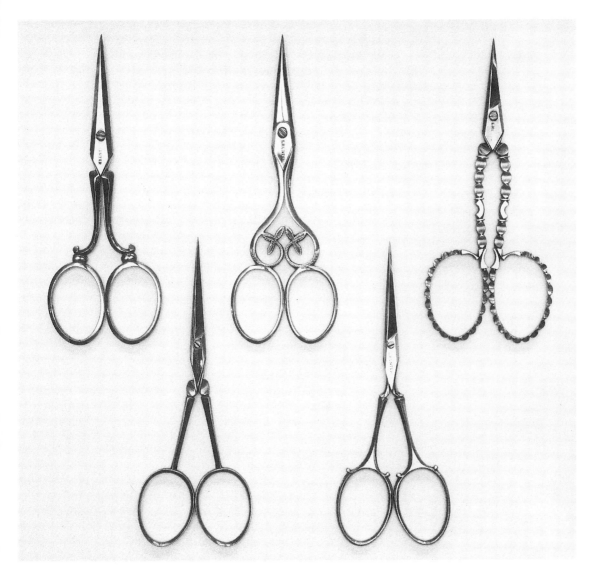

22 *Hand-forged scissors displayed at* The Great Exhibition, *1851,* Sheffield City Museums

blades were of identical hardness one would yield in use and be blunted by the other; the marks can be found by opening the scissors fully and examining the area near the pivot for a number or letter. Bows and shanks were filed into the chosen pattern by another highly skilled man and then hardened. Blades were ground and, as in the needle and pin industries, the men's health suffered and few lived to reach forty years of age until flues were introduced in the 1850s. After the screw was made, the blades were set true for cutting, the screw secured and the edges set with fine hones. Women and boys were employed for the finishing processes and every pair of scissors was tested by hand to ensure it cut the full length of the blade.

Sheffield City Museum has a very fine collection of hand-filed scissors in pristine condition made by one manufacturer to display at The Great Exhibition of 1851. While few of the designs and ornamentations on the tens of thousands of exhibits could be commended, these scissors were the epitome of superb British craftsmanship. There are more than a hundred pairs, some simple and elegant, but the majority with exuberant and fanciful motifs worked into the shanks and bows, including crowns, coats of arms, cherubs, animals, fish and birds. Bird scissors were a particular favourite and were made in abundance from 1830–70. The design continued until 1914 and a few pairs may date from after 1920, but

23 *Hand-forged scissors displayed at* The Great Exhibition, *1851*, Sheffield City Museums

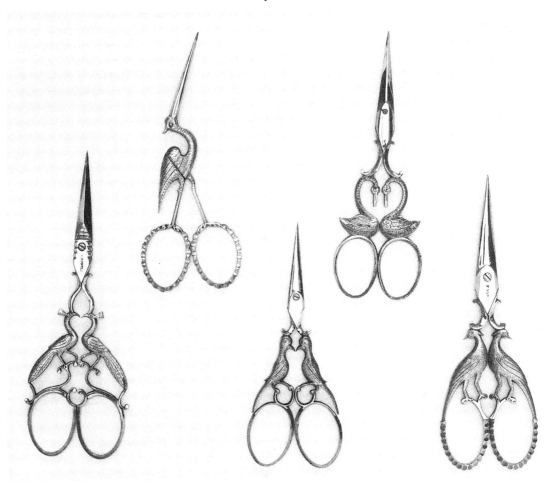

few surviving examples of decorative scissors are British made (figs 22, 23).

Another type of bird scissor, for embroidery, was made in various sizes in the shape of a stork. The idea may have originated in the Far East or Northern Europe and is still made today. Similar designs had a church with the spire as blades, a pierrot with a sword, or a huntsman with a gun. A free-standing stork with a flattened bill was probably a ribbon threader.

In 1835 it was considered necessary for the lady of the house to have six pairs of scissors: a large pair for cutting out, a medium pair for common use, one small pair with rounded points, another with sharper points for cutting out patterns on muslin, lace scissors with a flat knob on one of the points, and a pair of buttonhole scissors. Lace scissors had been introduced about 1830 for Carrickmacross work, in which a pattern on card was covered with net and then muslin, a

24 *Nineteenth-century buttonhole scissors*, Sheffield City Museums

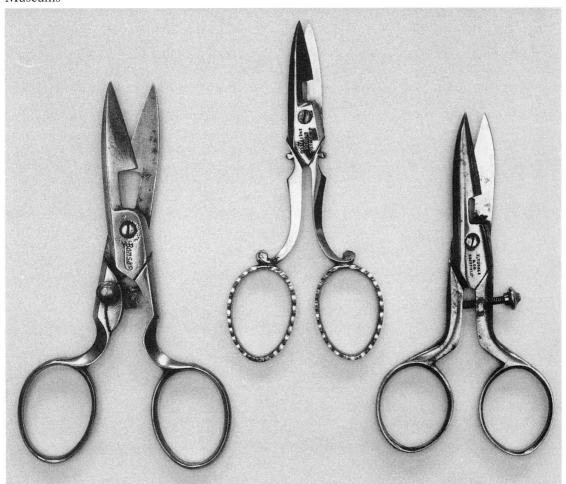

thread was oversewn to outline the design and the surplus muslin cut away leaving the flowers and leaves applied to the net. Although buttonhole scissors (fig 24) were available from 1800, many people preferred a sharp chisel blade set into a wooden or bone handle (fig 19f) or a small penknife, which could serve a similar purpose.

Before 1850 most Sheffield-made scissors were only marked with the maker's name. Subsequently 'Sheffield' was often, but not always, added. A few scissors made elsewhere were fraudulently stamped 'Sheffield' to take advantage of the good name. 'Made in England' was used after 1890.

Between 1780–1900 scissors made in Salisbury, Wiltshire, were stamped 'Sarum', the old name for the city. From the seventeenth century there had been a thriving industry which used local iron and charcoal. John Aubry (1626–97) described it as 'Salisbury, ever famous for the manufacture of razors, scissors and knives', but unfortunately very little information was recorded and few examples are known. The Salisbury and South Wiltshire Museum have some good quality pairs dated between 1850–90, including embroidery scissors with blades in the shape of the spire of the Cathedral and a beautiful pair in a steel sheath engraved with local views. No cutlers remained in business after 1914.

Many scissors were sold with a sheath to protect the delicate points. Shagreen, an expensive, grainy leather (not always sharkskin) dyed green, was fashionable in the late eighteenth and early nineteenth centuries. There were also beautiful sheaths of French enamels and silver-gilt with matching scissors. British silver scissors, with steel blades made in Sheffield and the silver handles made in Birmingham, had silver sheaths but were rarely hallmarked because they were too light in weight. Some inexpensive scissors were sold with a cardboard cover, and drapers' shop assistants kept their own pair hanging from the waist in a leather case.

Scissors were made in Spain, Italy and other European countries, but it was from France, and later Germany, that large numbers were exported to Britain. Between 1790–1830 scissors were among the novelties made of mother-of-pearl in the Palais Royal area of Paris but much of this output was no more than decorative toys; neither the solid, pearl-handled scissors, nor those with pearl glued onto metal handles, were of practical value and would break under the slightest pressure. Among other Palais Royal needlework accessories made of pearl, and sometimes decorated with a blue and gold pansy or a shield, were thimbles, needlecases, thread winders and bodkins. Mother-of-pearl was also used by the Indians and Chinese for needlework accessories but the decorations they used were very different from the work of French craftsmen.

Germany had a long association with scissor making, but cheap scissors were not exported in sufficient numbers to threaten the British market until the 1880s. They were made using hot dies to

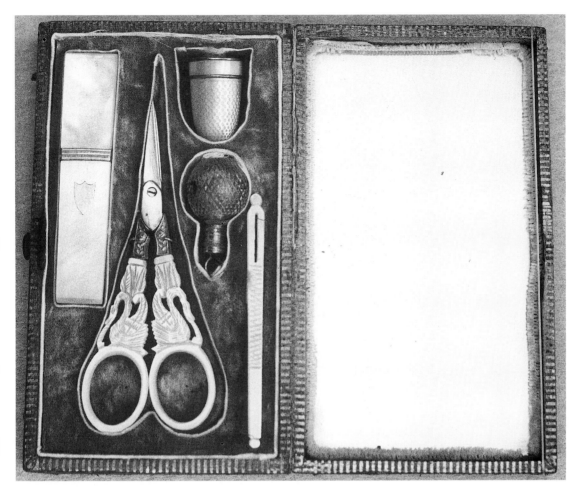

25 *Needlework case with mother-of-pearl fittings. French, 1800–30 with label – 'Balon Fabr: de Necessaire. Palais Royal No 161 A Paris'*, Sheffield City Museums

forge the complete shape, which required very little hand work to smooth the edges and sharpen the blades. The dies were expensive to produce and were only cost-effective if the shapes were simpler than hand-filed examples and produced in vast quantities. Popular designs between 1890–1920 copied many ideas from Britain and France, expecially birds, animals, insects, fish, soldiers, characters from fables and innumerable floral shapes. Unless marked, it is unwise to attribute the country of origin with certainty, although the majority of pairs came from Germany.

So-called Chinese embroidery scissors with very large bows and short, fine blades have been made since ancient times in the Far East and are still sold today. Dagger-shaped tools with bows arranged vertically are known as Persian scissors, but many intended to double as paper-knives were made in Sheffield during the nine-teenth century (figs 19i and j).

It is possible to identify hand-filed scissors, as the files can reach into all the crevices to produce a really smooth finish which is impossible by any other method, making the inner surface of a decorative scroll or bow should be as perfect as the outer edge. Once the rough shape was forged, all subsequent processes were worked by hand and it made little difference to the cost to produce a few dozen or many thousands of one design. As it was in the interest of the manufacturer to entice his customers with a large range of patterns, the number of filed scissors with identical designs may not be great. To distinguish scissors which were hot-forged using dies and then ground, consider the decoration. It will be less crisp than hand-filed examples, although still attractive, but the crevices will be unpolished and rough unless disguised, after 1900, by nickel plating. It is usually possible to discern the line where the two halves of the die came together, especially on the bows, and sometimes there are marks left by the grinding wheel or a nick where it slipped (fig 19a). Cold stamping was a cheaper method, but it could only produce very shallow decoration (fig 19b). Some cheap scissors were cast, and although satisfactory when new they soon became blunt. The shapes are heavy, the parting line from the die will certainly be visible and some scissors may have a pitted, orange-peel appearance. Many cast scissors were fitted into inexpensive sewing boxes from 1900–40.

Old scissors in good condition are not common; they were too useful to lie idle, and most were used until they broke.

CHAPTER 4

Pins

From the earliest times until the nineteenth century, large quantities of pins were used to fasten garments. The origin of the pin can be traced back to the use of a thorn or fishbone by primitive man; by the Bronze Age there were sometimes complexly-designed metal spikes and the Romans had hand-forged pins with elaborate heads. The use of pins on clothing declined once other fastenings were mass-produced, but in 1830 they were still recommended for baby clothes, together with a pincushion, as part of the layette.

A guild of pinners was established in London in 1356 and by the fifteenth century several other towns in Britain had pin-makers and guilds, but the production of good quality wire was a problem and large quantities of fine pins were imported from France. In 1483 Richard III attempted to boost the home market by prohibiting the importation of pins, but was not successful. Catherine Howard, wife of Henry VIII, has been credited with introducing brass pins to England in 1543; certainly in that year the King made a step towards controlling the quality of pins: 'No person shall put to sale any pinnes but only such as shall be double headed and have the heads soldered fast to the shank of the pinnes, well smoothed, the shank well shapen, the point well and round filed, canted and sharpened'. In spite of various attempts in Britain to improve the quality and quantity of brass and iron wire it continued to be imported until this was prohibited in 1662, and the industry was not really viable until 1700, when the areas around Gloucester and Bristol became centres of manufacture.

It is probable that a pin made from two pieces of wire, one for the shank and another with two or three coils for the head, was first made in the mid sixteenth century and continued until 1830. If these pins are attached to a dated document, an approximate age can be assumed. It is from such sources that experts have concluded that the dating of individual pins made from two pieces of wire is almost impossible, as the standard of workmanship does not give reliable evidence. During the late eighteenth century some spirally wound globular heads were replaced by a conical shape which used wire of a smaller diameter with up to five turns.

Pin making was similar to needle making and almost as expensive; at the end of the fifteenth century when a sheep sold for twenty pence, pins, pointed individually on a pinner's bone, cost four pence a hundred. The processes necessary to make a pin in 1776 were described by Adam Smith, the Scottish economist, in *An Inquiry into the Nature and Causes of the Wealth of Nations*. Wire was first reduced to the correct gauge by hand drawing, cut into lengths and pointed at both ends on a grinding wheel, then cut and pointed several more times until the required length was obtained. The head was a close spiral made on a long wire and cut into lengths of two or three turns. A number of coils were put into a tray, or the worker's apron, and four headless shanks placed into a holder. By pushing this through the coils a head was picked up on each of them. The heads were secured with pressure by a machine. Most pins were tinned before being 'barrelled' in a manually turned bran tub to polish them. This lengthy process, with one craftsman undertaking eighteen distinct operations, produced twenty pins per man per day. Smith explained how re-distribution of labour, which detailed one craftsman to each task, increased production to 4,800 pins per man per day. The pin industry is quoted as a milestone in industrial progress.

There were various attempts to make a one-piece pin. In 1797 Timothy Harris took out a patent for a pinhead made from molten lead. In 1817 an American, Seth Hunt, patented an upsetting machine which made pins with a head, shaft and point. This was bought by Kirby, Beard and Company of Gloucester, but was not successful as it could only make pins from soft wire, and so the harder, spirally-wound type continued to be sold. It was another American, Lemuel W. Wright, who changed the British pin making industry. In 1824 he patented a machine which forced the head up from the shank and formed it in one movement, producing 40–50 solid-headed pins per minute. Wright set up his business in London and later moved to Stroud, Gloucestershire, but after a short time he sold out to Daniel Foote Tayler, who adapted the machine to make 170 pins per minute. It is probable that he sold the first solid-headed pins in London in 1833. In 1840 the company was sold and moved to Birmingham, but it continued to trade as D.F. Tayler and used their 'Dorcas' trademark. In 1860 a booklet, *Useful Arts*, explained how solid-headed pins were made and illustrated the various stages in manufacture with actual examples. Pin making was fully automatic by 1880. Newey, founded in 1798 to make shoe buckles, absorbed D.F. Tayler in 1934, and their catalogue of that year illustrated various pin papers and boxes which bore a portrait of the young Queen Victoria – which shows how unwise it is to attribute a date of manufacture from the packaging! As Newey Goodman Limited they now make pins from brass, carbon and stainless steel, and recommend 'Dorcas' pins for dressmaking. Needles made by John James & Son, Charles Horner's thimbles and an Irish linen were also called 'Dorcas'.

Although pin making in Gloucester gradually declined, there are a number of pin-making machines at Gloucester Folk Museum,

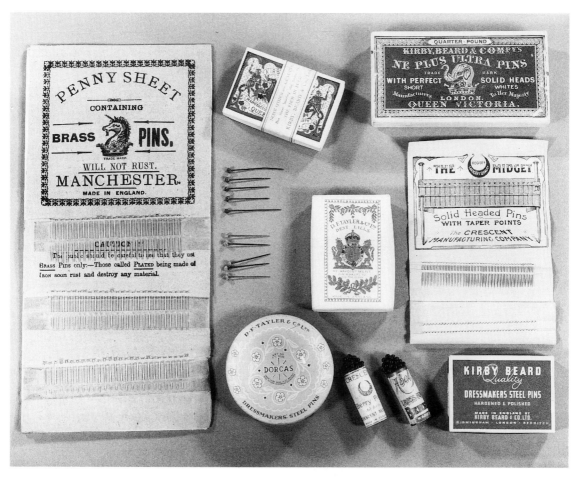

26 *Pins.   a A pin sheet, c.1900   b, c, g Pin boxes with*
labels that indicate a Victorian date but they may be much later
d 'The Crescent' was the trade mark of a wholesaler,
Olney Amsden, not a manufacturer   e After 1950   f Berry or
toilet pins in black for mourning cost 2d per packet in 1929
h, i Light and dark hariffes headed with seeds

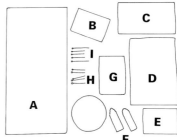

displayed on the top floor of an old building that was once a pin-
making workshop.

Most lace pins were, and still are made of fine brass wire. They
sold for 200 a penny in about 1880. If the head came off, lace makers
would repair the pin by replacing it with a bead, sealing wax or a
cleavers seed (goose-grass). The seeds were soaked, in milk for a
light colour or vinegar for dark, and when swollen the rough skin
was rubbed off and the smooth seed put on the shank, where it dried
and tightened. They were known as hariffes (fig 26h and i).

In the early nineteenth century the *Spectator* published a long
article on possible sources of the term 'pin money' without reaching

any conclusion. There was some evidence it may have originated in the sixteenth century, but it might date from even earlier. One suggestion came from a custom in the reign of Henry VIII (1509–47) when pin makers were only allowed to sell their wares in open shops on the 1st and 2nd of January each year, and ladies flocked to buy them with pin money. Another idea concerned Charles I (1626–49), who renewed import restrictions on pins and received £500 per year in return, which he gave to his wife, Henrietta Maria, as part of her income. There was also the practice of adding a few extra coins for good service when an account was settled as 'Pin money for your wife'. Whatever the truth of the matter, once pins became cheap and plentiful pin money was understood to be a very small sum, earned or saved for incidental expenses.

There was strong competition to market pins attractively and by 1800 the majority were sold 'stuck' in coloured paper. Women and children used a comb-shaped tool which was passed through a shallow tray containing loose pins. With one sweep it collected a pin between each tooth, then with a deft flick of the wrist a complete row of pins was pushed into crimped paper. Pin papers sold for a penny or less and were made until the 1930s (fig 26a and d).

By 1840 pins (and needles) were sold in decorative card and metal boxes. Lewis, Wright & Bayliss, in a catalogue from 1886, offered to label various containers with a shop's name and address; for example, 'John Wood Tenterden', 'W. Coads Uxbridge', or 'W. Morgan Shaftesbury – linen and woollen draper, hatter and tailor'. These names must not be confused with that of the maker. In Kirby Beard's list of 1903 there were 38 distinct packages, each available with various sizes and types of pin. The 'Ne Plus Ultra' could be supplied in Regina, London, Crown or Celebrated Quality in fancy metal boxes in crystallised, diamond, spotted or art metal. Two years later a wholesaler, Jeremiah Rotherham, offered over fifty varieties of papers, packets, books, boxes and barrels of pins. The barrels were small, rough, wooden containers with a label at one end which retailed at a penny each and were also used for boot and trouser buttons. Fancy metal and card boxes of pins and needles were sold until 1939.

Some holders for pins, including pincushions, were never intended for needlework. From 1600–1930 large decorative pincushions were kept in dressing rooms for toilet and hat pins. Silk cushions, decorated with a design of pins to commemorate a birth or wedding, were made from the seventeenth to the early nineteenth centuries and there has been a recent revival. Similar, but cruder, examples in felt or woollen cloth, decorated with large pins and beads, were made by servicemen during the second half of the nineteenth century and in the First World War. Charming pin balls, meant to hang from the waist, were made in the eighteenth century from very fine silk knitted or woven into a pattern which often included the date. Some of these were made by children in Quaker

27 *Decorative but impractical pincushions made in the*
second half of nineteenth century.   a Patchwork, nineteenth-
century templates were made of wood, card or tin-plate
b Soldier's work, late nineteenth-early twentieth century
c North American Indian-type beadwork   d Welsh beaded cushion,
National Museum of Wales (Welsh Folk Museum)

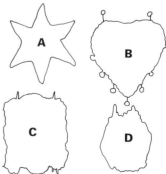

schools. During the eighteenth and early nineteenth centuries ladies could keep a few pins in a pin poppet, a small box of wood, bone or ivory with a tightly-fitting lid and maybe a little pincushion inside. From the late eighteenth century until the 1840s there was a fashion to make pin (and emery) cushions from a piece of silk printed to commemorate a special occasion or political opinion. A print which showed the emblem for the Society for the Abolition of Slavery – a kneeling negro in manacles and the legend 'Am I not a man and a brother?' – may be contemporary with the Wedgwood Jasper Ware medallions with an identical design which were distributed in Britain and the USA between 1787–91. A print on the death of Princess Charlotte, 1817, and another with Robert Peel's Repeal of the Corn Laws, 1846, were both popular, as were small maps between 1800–25. There was a revival from 1900–30 when cigarette manufactureres gave away small, polychrome, woven silk pictures.

Really practical pincushions, usually plain and fairly large, were either free-standing or attached to a clamp (discussed in Chapter 7). They were stuffed with sheep's wool, cotton wool, sawdust or bran and, if weighted, contained lead shot, a piece of metal or a brick.

Throughout the last 200 years ladies have acquired numerous small pincushions of little or no practical value, but nevertheless quite enchanting. There were probably more pincushions collected than any other needlework accessory and ladies' magazines were continually publishing ideas for new novelties, including the 60-piece patchwork star designed in 1897 for Queen Victoria's Diamond Jubilee. Averil Colby in *Pincushions* (Batsford, 1975) attempted to arrange the various types under suitable headings, but as there are so many variations this is almost impossible. Dating any pincushion is very uncertain and although comparing them with popular crafts and fashions in fabrics might be helpful, it could be misleading. For example, painted ribbons were popular in the early nineteenth century and at a similar time talented, amateur water-colourists were decorating white silk pincushions with delicate views and floral bouquets, but the painted silk playing-card cushions came much later; tartan silks were fashionable between 1830–50, but as a pincushion needs such a small scrap of material off-cuts might have been kept for many years before they were used.

The beginning of the nineteenth century saw the introduction of small, disc-shaped pincushions, probably first made in France and very popular in Britain. Although small, usually less than 2 in (50mm) in diameter, some were kept in sewing boxes and actually used. The ends were made from plain or decorated ivory, bone, mother-of-pearl, tortoise-shell or wood and joined by a narrow velvet or silk ribbon. One disc with ivory ends has the date 1812 marked with tiny coil-headed pins, less than $\frac{1}{2}$ in (12mm) in length and known as lills or lillikins. Discs were less fashionable after 1840 but many were made to the end of the century. Variations from the circular shape were crude rectangles or representations of house-

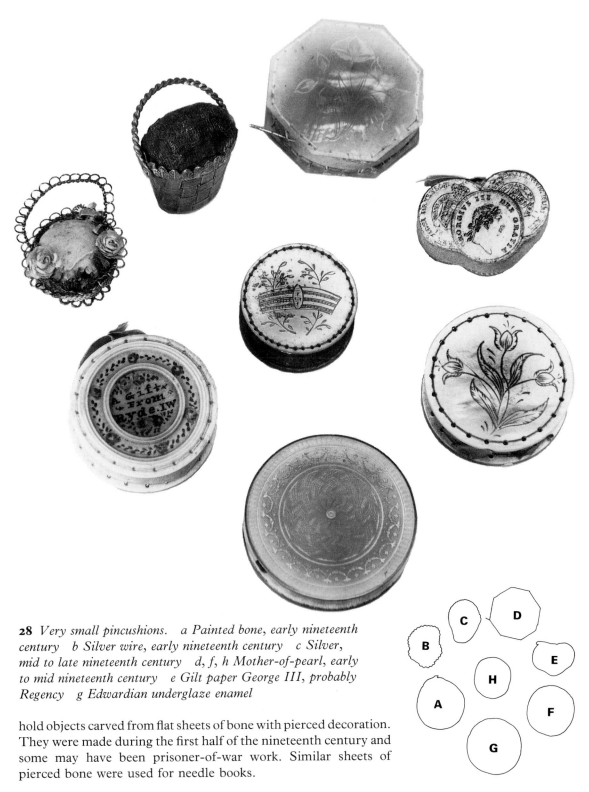

28 *Very small pincushions.   a Painted bone, early nineteenth century   b Silver wire, early nineteenth century   c Silver, mid to late nineteenth century   d, f, h Mother-of-pearl, early to mid nineteenth century   e Gilt paper George III, probably Regency   g Edwardian underglaze enamel*

hold objects carved from flat sheets of bone with pierced decoration. They were made during the first half of the nineteenth century and some may have been prisoner-of-war work. Similar sheets of pierced bone were used for needle books.

Souvenir pin discs, needle books and paperweights decorated with a coloured print under glass were made between 1850–75. A picture was glued to the underside, a few features such as the windows scraped away, and the whole backed with foil which showed through as highlights when viewed from the front (colour illustration 11). Later in the century sepia photographs were substituted for the gay prints.

Some pincushions were very small and were probably more ornamental than useful, but they were free-standing and may have been kept on the mantleshelf or side table with a few useful pins. Little metal baskets with a velvet or silk cushion were popular for a time in the early nineteenth century. Lucky shoes of metal, ceramic or fabric were made throughout Victorian times and into the next century, as were the small animals which held a pincushion on their back. The minute cushions fitted into sea-shells and nuts were really too small to use but provided a meagre income for the cottagers that made them.

The majority of pincushions made entirely of fabric, or of fabric on a foundation of card, were probably made at home as a pastime. A design popular since the early 1800s was made from two circles of card, each covered with material and sewn together so the pins could be pushed into the edge (cardboard milk-bottle tops were sometimes used as a foundation between 1920–55). Miniature buttoned mattresses and over-stuffed cushions coincided with similar styles in upholstery. From 1880–1910 pincushions were fashioned into realistic shapes using patterns printed in journals: jockey caps, fans, butterflies, flowers, balls and all manner of ingenious ideas had pins stuck into every seam (colour illustration 10).

Pincushions are still made today and many old styles have been revived.

CHAPTER 5

Measures, emeries and waxers

Measures

In 1494 Henry VII ordered that every town and city in England should be sent a King's Standard of each measure (and weight) for comparison. From 1640 a standard brass measure was chained in every market place and after 1670 measures in public use had to be officially stamped. In 1835 inspectors were appointed to check measures and a few years later it became illegal to sell any yard measure without metal ends.

At one time there were two units of measurement in Britain: the ell (45 inches/1.145 metres) and the yard (36 inches/0.914 metre). During the eighteenth century some shops, including drapers, used a wooden ell divided by brass nails two and a quarter inches apart. The nail was a useful size for short lengths and, as it was a fraction of a yard, it was marked on some yard sticks as well. The yard was preferred for domestic use and divided into inches or half-yard, quarter, half-quarter and nail, indicated by Y, HY, Q, HQ and N. By 1800 the yard had largely replaced the ell but, in spite of inches being increasingly preferred, in 1905 brass measures calibrated in nails were still available for shop keepers.

Most households had a yard stick, and until tape measures were manufactured in the early nineteenth century, a piece of tape, ribbon or parchment was set against this stick and calibrated in ink to provide an approximate measurement.

From the 1890s a few yardsticks were used to carry advertising and after the turn of the century tape measures were also used, but neither was very popular. Most of the fabric, and even paper, tapes which carried advertisements were probably made in the 1920s and 1930s; for example, 'Scotts Porage Oats 2 lbs for 10d' and 'Use Matchless Metal Polish'. Since 1950 there have been occasional plastic advertising tapes such as that for 'Marvel Milk'.

There were some very stout tapes made with slogans, for example 'Viyella' and 'Paton's Wool', which were probably given to shops for their own use. Another tape, used by professional sock knitters, was only 12 in (30cm) long with calibrations for the leg, welt, foot and the finished size.

The container, made to hold a fabric tape wound on to a spindle, gave scope for decoration but it is unlikely any were made before

1800. The earliest examples, almost certainly made in France for fitted work boxes, had frail ribbons a metre in length calibrated in centimetres or marked $\frac{1}{2}$, $\frac{1}{4}$, $\frac{1}{8}$, $\frac{1}{16}$, $\frac{1}{32}$; the metre was used before Napoleon made it statutory in 1799. The majority were in cylindrical or barrel-shaped containers and made of ivory or bone with simple decoration. By the 1820s considerable numbers were imported into Britain, but they declined for a time when Queen Adelaide, wife of William IV, attempted to boost the home market. Most early ribbons had a small bone or ivory bar to prevent them disappearing inside when re-wound but a few, especially in fine quality filigree silver and enamel cases, had a well-made loop. By 1830 most tapes were hand-written in inches for the British market and hand work continued for another thirty years, in spite of the increased use of printed measures.

A tape measure in a fancy case was a favourite gift, inexpensive but useful. From the accession of Queen Victoria in 1837 to the present day, large numbers have been imported from France, Germany and the Far East as well as being made in Britain (figs 29 and 30). Very few tape measures in holders were home-made, with

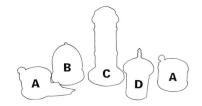

29 *Wooden tape measures. a Wooden holder with cranked handle and strong tape, c.1850 b Ebony?, mid nineteenth century c Scottish souvenir emery, tape measure and waxer d Rosewood from a fitted work box, early to mid nineteenth century,* York Castle Museum

30 *Tape measures. a Wood, nineteenth century b Celluloid, 1920 c Metal, 1880 d Vegetable ivory e Metal, 1890 f Metal, 1890 g Wood, 1860+ h Early Tunbridge Ware i Tape with emery cushion in vegetable ivory j Wood and steel studding, before 1840 k Mother-of-pearl from workbox, 1840–80 l Silver from work box, c.1830 m Ivory from work box, c.1830*

the possible exception of those with embroidered calibrations. Most were manfactured or assembled as a cottage industry or in small workshops.

Two large types of nut were used to make needlework accessories, including holders for tape measures, emeries, waxers, cotton barrels, pincushions and thimbles. The coquilla nut came from a Brazilian palm tree and was well-known in Europe as a material for snuff boxes in the eighteenth century. The shell was turned, carved and frequently pierced, and may be recognized by its ginger-brown colour. Many more needlework accessories were made from the kernel of the corozo nut, another palm with very large seeds. It was known as vegetable or mutton ivory which described the texture very well, although it darkened to a honey colour with age, it was used for a pincushion on colour illustration 10. Vegetable ivory was known from the 1700s and much used between 1850–1900 for multiple accessories such as an emery and waxer or a pincushion with a holder for a reel of thread. A few workbox fittings were also made from it, but it was always an inexpensive material.

Until 1890 the majority of tape measures were rewound manually by turning the spindle, sometimes with the help of a tiny, cranked handle. Although the spring recoil was invented in the 1860s it was rarely used until the latter years of the century and not common until after 1900.

Great changes took place in the industry after 1890 when metal and plastic could be moulded cheaply into realistic shapes. There was no limit to the ingenious ideas that proliferated – tasteless but fun. Before 1940 many novelties were manufactured in Germany. The abbreviation DRGM, 'Deutsches Reich Gebrauch Muster' is the provisional patent mark and 'Ges Gesch' the copyright design mark, both introduced about 1890. Since 1950 the majority have been made in Hong Kong from plastic.

Emeries

Emery is a variety of corundum and although sand could be used as a cheap substitute, this scratched rather than polished. It was beneficial to polish needles by pushing them in and out of a cushion containing an abrasive before commencing fine work, as this removed any traces of rust. Emery holders were fitted into some work boxes. Decorative containers could be purchased separately or the powder bought at an ironmongers and made into a little cushion at home. Emery cushions are always very small, heavier for their size than a pincushion and, if squeezed, give a rasping sound.

Emery holders in work boxes were cylindrical with a small, fabric-covered hole in the side or base. An empty emery case can be distinguished from one that held a tape measure, as one has a round hole while the other has a slit. Disc-shaped cushions with decorated ends made of mother-of-pearl, ivory or bone and joined by ribbon were made during the first half of the nineteenth century for emery as well as pins. Knitted or fabric emeries in the shape of a strawberry, with the seeds beaded or embroidered, were made during the eighteenth and nineteenth centuries. Instructions for making these and other emery cushions were included in *Weldon's*

31 *Moulded metal and plastic tape measures, 1890–1930,*
Worthing Museum

32 *Emery cushions of horn and velvet, velvet and silk, beadwork, canvas work and crochet with a box of emery powder. All nineteenth century*

Practical Needlework in the 1890s, but by this time they were seldom used as needles were so cheap it was easier to take a new one.

Waxers

Until the mid nineteenth century linen, cotton and silk threads were drawn through wax before use to help prevent fraying and give them

33 *Waxers.   a Block of beeswax   b Set with silver thimble and white wax, mid nineteenth century   c Tunbridge stick ware emery and waxer   d Waxer and pin poppet of ivory, early to mid nineteenth century   e, f Mother-of-pearl from work boxes, 1840–80*

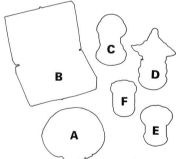

greater strength. Dark-coloured beeswax obtained from hives was moulded into blocks for everyday use. Decorative holders were available from the late eighteenth century onwards and were popular until the mercerisation of cotton and linen made wax unnecessary. Few were made after 1860. Although most holders held natural beeswax, a light-coloured, refined, white wax was more suitable for light-coloured fabrics and was sometimes sold in little cakes decorated with fancy papers. Black wax was used by tailors and cobblers. Many wax holders or waxers do not have their original contents; they have been replaced by a piece of candle.

CHAPTER 6

Thimbles

Thimbles have been treasured for centuries and more has been written about them than any other needlework tool. Though they are not numerous in museums, there are thousands of avid collectors with their own societies devoted to these charming objects. The following information is only a brief guide to the subject and purely decorative examples have been omitted because they were not intended for practical use. Several excellent reference books are listed in the bibliography.

During archaeological excavations ancient thimbles made of bronze, bone and ivory have been found. They are either ring-shaped or have the more familiar dome with irregular, hand-punched indentations – 'knurling'. During the sixteenth century brass thimbles were imported and a few of silver made in Britain; in 1693 the first cast brass ones were made in London by a Dutchman, John Lofting.

At the beginning of the eighteenth century most ladies used a brass thimble, although silver ones were being made in increasing numbers. Very few have survived – the cheap, brass articles were discarded when a hole developed and many silver ones were also thrown away for the same reason, although it was possible to have these repaired by a jeweller. Early thimbles seldom bear any marks except the maker's name. The majority of thimbles from this period were short and heavy for their size, had a pronounced curved top and were rimless. Individually punched knurling gradually changed to a pattern which was applied several rows at a time. Thimbles were either cast complete and finished on a lathe or made up from two pieces of metal.

During the second half of the eighteenth century the deep-drawing process which revolutionized the industry was discovered, thus brass and silver thimbles could be made more quickly and cheaply. A disc of metal of the required size was pressed into the basic shape by machine and the knurling added in one action, after which further decoration by hand or machine was possible. The deep-drawing process made elegant, slender thimbles, but the metal was thin and weak. To overcome this problem some makers fixed a steel top to brass and silver thimbles; it can be identified from the colour of the metal. From about 1775 some silver thimbles were

"Dorcas" Thimbles.

To avoid confusion, please note that the sizes for "Dorcas" and Hall-marked Silver Thimbles are somewhat larger than the sizes used for ordinary Thimbles.

| Design A. PLAIN. | Design B. ENGRAVED. | Design D. DAISY. | Design E. DIAMOND. Rd. No 73626. | Design F. STAR. |

| Design G. LOUISE. | Design H. PERSIAN. | Design J. FLORA. | Design K. SHELL. Rd. No. 210799. | Design L. PRINCESS MAY. Rd. No. 210800. |

STERLING SILVER.

34 *Dorcas Thimbles, 1900* Newey Goodman Ltd

decorated with lines or trails of leaves on the border below the knurling and some had rims.

The artistic designs of the Regency period became more flamboyant after 1840 and ten years later very ornate silver thimbles were made in hundreds of different designs, using a new method of manufacture in which the flat metal was die-stamped before being rolled into shape and soldered. It was cheap, but the finished result was only as good as the die; worn out dies produced poor quality thimbles. Although it cost more than brass, silver was not expensive; in 1895 wholesale drapers sold silver thimbles from six to fifteen shillings a dozen and in *The Army and Navy Stores Catalogue*, 1928, plain silver ones were one shilling and threepence, engraved two shillings (10p) each, retail.

Dating Victorian silver thimbles can be difficult. They were made in a wide range of designs and proportions which varied with the maker's preference; for example, although there was a fashion for tall thimbles early in the century, some were manufactured after 1900. It was a similar story with the rim: some makers had them, others did not. However thimbles with all-over knurling were not made before 1850 and were popular until the 1920s. They had patterns of daisies, shells, stars and the square 'waffle' pattern, which was re-introduced from earlier hand-made examples. Makers were always inventing new designs and patenting some of them.

Before 1890 very few silver thimbles were hall-marked, but after 1900 most were. In Britain silver objects had to be assayed to guarantee quality, although certain small items were exempt because their low value did not warrant the cost. A hall-mark will identify the year an object was assayed, the town where this was done and usually the initials of the maker; booklets to explain the marks are available from jewellers. Well-known makers of thimbles included James Fenton, Henry (later Samuel) Foskett, Henry Griffiths, Charles Horner and Charles May.

The problem with all silver thimbles was that the soft metal was easily damaged by a steel needle. Various attempts were made to solve the problem satisfactorily, and it was Charles Horner of Halifax, who discovered a really practical solution – a thimble made in three parts with a layer of steel sandwiched between two layers of silver. It was patented in 1884, called 'The Dorcas', and sold for two shillings and sixpence ($12\frac{1}{2}$p). Each thimble was stamped with 'Pat.' and, where applicable, the registered design number. They were sold in small blue cardboard boxes lined with blue velvet and labelled: 'The Dorcas thimble, Sterling Silver. Made in three parts the inner and outer being silver and the intermediate steel giving a resistance to wear not obtained in silver alone'. In 1905 improved production reduced the price to two shillings; the thimbles were stamped 'Dorcas C.H.' and the label amended to offer replacement if rendered useless from any cause. They were very popular with needlewomen and manufactured in large quantities. In 1928 plain designs cost three shillings, while fancy were three shillings and ninepence. Between 1945 and the end of production in 1948, the label included the word 'Guarantee' and the boxes were lined with white felt (fig 38h). All the patterns used for 'Dorcas' thimbles were also used by Horner's on their thimbles of solid silver – it is very important to observe the marks. Horner's idea of a reinforced thimble was a good one; although 'Dorcas' remained the leader, Henry Griffith made 'The Dreamer' and Walker & Hall 'The Dura'.

Some other metals were marked to imply they were silver. Serviceable thimbles may be marked 'nickel-silver', 'German silver' or 'E.P.N.S.' (electro-plated nickel silver). These alloys were also used between 1890–1930 for thimbles which had an additonal gadget for cutting thread or threading a needle, and for the strange

35 *Silver and brass thimbles, late nineteenth to early twentieth century. a, b Brass c Silver interior and rim, plated 'gold' outside d, e, f, h, i Silver g Silver, free gift from James Walker Ltd 1920–39 (City of Salford Museum and Art Galleries)*

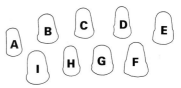

thimble shaped like a finger with a nail, although the latter was also made in sliver. Thimbles for tambour work are described in Chapter 10.

Brass thimbles were occasionally decorated but rarely as elaborately as silver (fig 35a and b). For really hard wear there was steel, but this was never ornamented. Large brass and steel thimbles without a top are used by tailors who prefer to push the needle with the side of the thimble. Between 1890 and 1939 many combinations of metal, plastic and enamel linings were tried in an attempt to make brass and steel thimbles more pleasant to use. In 1895 silver-plated steel sold at four pence three farthings each retail and in 1900 enamelled brass cost seven and sixpence (about 37p) a gross wholesale.

Before 1890 thimbles were not marked with the size but sold as large, womens, maids or childs. After 1900 thimbles of all materials, even plastic, had a size number impressed on them – the higher the number the smaller the thimble, from 00 to 9.

In the nineteenth century girls at Charity Schools were expected to be able to sew and to knit their own stockings by the time they were five years old, while girls brought up in a family were taught to sew by their mothers, and everyone used a thimble. Although there were delightful silver thimbles made for children, the majority wore brass. This could be very unpleasant if the child had a sore finger, as it encouraged infection. About 1900 *Needlework for Student Teachers* by Amy Smith recommends 'Dorcas' thimbles for children, if there is sufficient money available; otherwise cheap brass thimbles for infants could be bought for one shilling and eightpence (less than 20p) a gross. This book gives a thimble drill for children aged three to five years: '1. Hold up your right hand. 2. Take up the thimble. 3. Put on finger. 4. Show'. Not all small thimbles were made for children; some were charms, some for dolls and at one time a thimble was one of the playing tokens in a Monopoly set.

Around 1900 the Prudential Insurance Company of America gave away brass thimbles embossed with its name. The idea spread and soon other firms were advertising on brass thimbles in Britain, especially makers of sewing threads and tea, including C.W.S (Co-operative Wholesale Society), Mazawattee and Blue Cross, followed a few years later by Brown's Pure Ales, Lutona Cocoa and others.

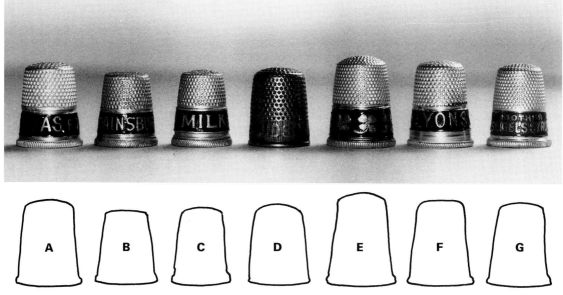

36 *Advertising thimbles, all aluminium except d, 1920s.*
a Gas for Economy   *b* Sainsbury's Teeth   *c* Diploma Milk
d Hudson's Soap *(brass)*   *e* Irish Linen emblem
f Lyons Cakes   *g* Mother Seigal's Syrup for Indigestion

There were also small sewing kits with a brass thimble for the lid advertising Hudson's Soap and C.W.S. Crumpsall Cream Crackers, which may have been given away as a special promotion or exchanged for tokens. Solid silver thimbles were offered by Lipton's Tea, Lifebuoy Soap, Quaker Oats, Hovis Bread (who produced a large range of items from 1910–39) and James Walker, the jewellers (fig 35g). Walkers had many branches between the wars and every November and December they gave each customer who spent more than five shillings (25p) a free gift which cost the firm fourpence halfpenny each (about 2p).

Aluminium was used by a few makers between 1918–39 to make cheap thimbles that were sometimes plated to resemble brass or silver. These can be identified by their light weight. Millions of aluminium thimbles for advertising were made during the same period and during the 1930s the leading manufacturer was Charles Iles of Birmingham. All the thimbles had the name of the product stamped into the coloured border and the list of brand names ran into hundreds. A handful of the names are still marketed – 'News of the World', 'Andrew's Liver Salts' and 'Nestles Milk', but what became of 'J. N. Side Spring Corsets', 'Gypsy Blacklead' or 'Sainsbury's Teeth'? All aluminium thimbles were soft and easily damaged, although those with a red or green glass top were slightly stronger.

Thimbles were made as souvenirs. One of silver, dated 'February 2nd 1829', commemorated a fire at York Minster. Silver and base metals were used for The Great Exhibition, 1851, and similar events. Royalty, castles, cathedrals, famous buildings and personalities have all found their way on to thimbles. Henry Griffiths of Leamington Spa made thimbles from 1856–1974 and popularized souvenirs during the 1930s. He was marketing a heavy silver thimble called 'The Spa' which sold for two shillings (10p), or a cheaper version for sixpence ($2\frac{1}{2}$p), which were adapted by the addition of a place name to attract customers at the seaside, large towns and some unusual places such as Chatham Dockyard and Croydon Airport.

For fine white work some ladies preferred an ivory thimble and a few were included in fitted workboxes, but they were never common and many so-called 'ivories' are not. The natural markings on real ivory form dark lines, but plastic can be deceptive.

Finding a substitute for ivory was a long-standing objective of nineteenth century inventors. In 1862 Alexander Parkes of Birmingham patented 'Parkesine' for making imitation ivory and mother-of-pearl but it was not successful. In 1866 the business was bought by Daniel Spill and in 1869 he produced 'Xylonite' and 'Ivorite', a substitute for 'Ivory, bone, horn, tortoise-shell, wood, marble, papier mâché and suitable for water-proofing fabrics and machine bearings' but, in spite of all this, it was not viable. Meanwhile in America the first useful plastic was invented by John Hyatt, who registered the name 'celluloid' in 1869. A subsidiary company was licensed in 1878 to make hollow articles, including thimbles. At first celluloid was no cheaper than the natural product, but the enormous demand for fashionable articles in ivory and the shortage of real tortoise-shell led to its gradual acceptance. Hyatt was also issued with a patent for making imitation ivory using ivory dust composition, but there is little evidence of what became of this. It may have been called 'Ivorine' but this name (sometimes spelt 'Ivorene') was also used by Charles Iles for his celluloid thimbles, 1900–25.

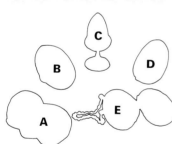

37 *Thimble cases. a Vegetable ivory, c.1850+   b Painted bone,
early nineteenth century   c Wooden acorn, early nineteenth
century   d, e Metal, 1890–1910,* York Castle Museum

Imitation ivory, made from celluloid, copied the graining of the
natural substance by putting sheets of various thickness in shades of
white and beige together, then bending and folding them under hot
rollers. Celluloid could be made in any colour, transparent or
opaque. 'Tortoiseshell' was made by mixing amber and brown while
the plastic was soft. Celluloid was firmly established in Britain and
elsewhere before 1880 and was used for various needlework tools
and accessories until the 1930s.

Bakelite (1909), the first of the artificial resins, was usually
mottled dark brown, green or red. Present day brightly-coloured
plastic thimbles are injection moulded thermoplastics.

Cheap thimbles were also made of Vulcanite, a hard black rubber
invented in 1855 by the Goodyear Rubber Company, USA. There
was a British patent to make various products, including thimbles,
in 1905, and another in 1908 for a thimble with a celluloid lining.
Vulcanite was used until the 1930s.

38 *Thimble cases.* *a Jeweller's case,* c.*1900* *b Tunbridge Ware*
c Tartan Ware *d Ebony and vegetable? ivory* *e Wood with*
child's thimble *f French needle and thimble case in beadwork*
'Le Roi VI7E' *g Silver cradle,* 1906 *h Dorcas box,* 1945–8
i Wood *j Red-stained ivory* c.1830 *k Wooden acorn with child's*
thimble

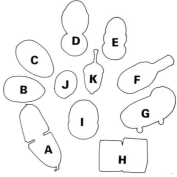

In the eighteenth century expensive thimbles had expensive cases, but very few have survived complete, and even later cases rarely contain their original thimbles. Throughout the nineteenth century quantities of charming thimble cases were made from every conceivable material. The majority were egg-shaped, but all manner of novelties were produced commercially and by hand. Tunbridge and Scottish souvenir wares were made over a long period and are difficult to date, but some ideas followed the fashions in other crafts and are probably contemporary with them. Real ivory, mother-of-pearl and tortoiseshell of good quality were purchased before 1840 in fancy goods shops; vegetable ivory could be bought until the end of the century. Thimbles displayed under glass domes, inside garish pyramids, or on a plush bed of roses are more likely to have come from a drapers after 1880. Hand-made shoes, hats, coal scuttles, etc. were sold at bazaars and probably made from patterns in *Weldon's Practical Needlework* and other journals; they can still be bought at similar events today.

Jewellers sold silver thimbles in functional cases (fig 38a).

A metal finger-guard or shield could be worn to prevent injury to the forefinger of the left hand, especially when hemming; these were usually, but not always, open at the top. Some decorative guards made of silver in the late eighteenth and early nineteenth centuries were sold in sets with a matching thimble. From 1900 to the present day, celluloid and later thermoplastic guards have been available in white, polychrome or tortoiseshell colours (fig 39 and colour illustration 12).

39 *Finger guards in silver, early nineteenth century.*
The decorated guard was sold with matching thimble (see colour illustration 12 for plastic guard), York Castle Museum

CHAPTER 7

Needlework clamps

Until about 1800 all yarns were sold in skeins and had to be wound into a ball or transferred on to a bobbin or flat winder before they could be used. Although this could be accomplished by two people without using any accessory, there were special devices made to hold the skein which enabled one person to work alone. Winding frames were in use during the sixteenth century or earlier; these were made from two pieces of wood forming a cross and set onto a spindle with a series of pegs to accommodate various sizes of skeins. Some were clamped to a chair or table, others were adapted into floor-standing, vertical winders. During the nineteenth century a special winder called a swift held any size of skein on expandable lattice arms which

40 *Wooden swift, second half of nineteenth century*

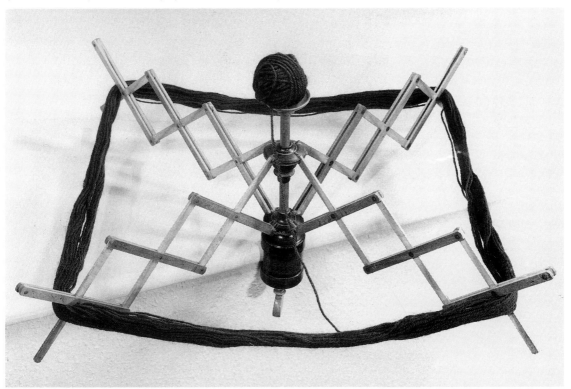

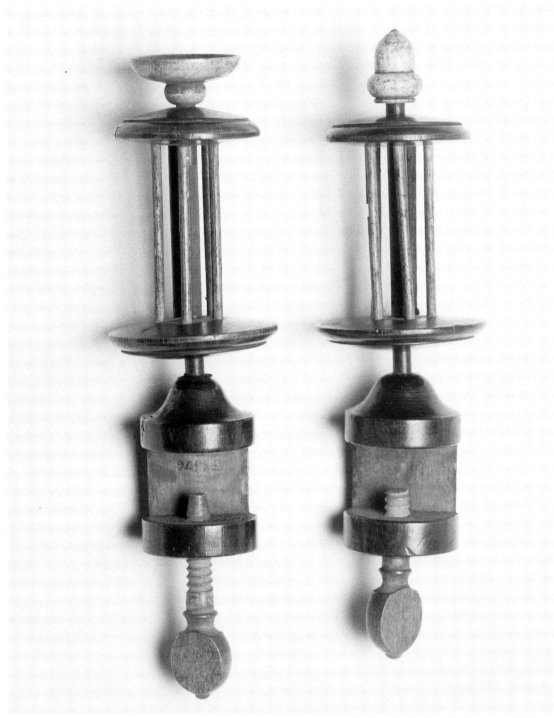

41 *Large pair of winding clamps 12 in (30 cm) high. Identical clamp shape to fig 40. Second half of nineteenth century,* Gloucester Folk Museum

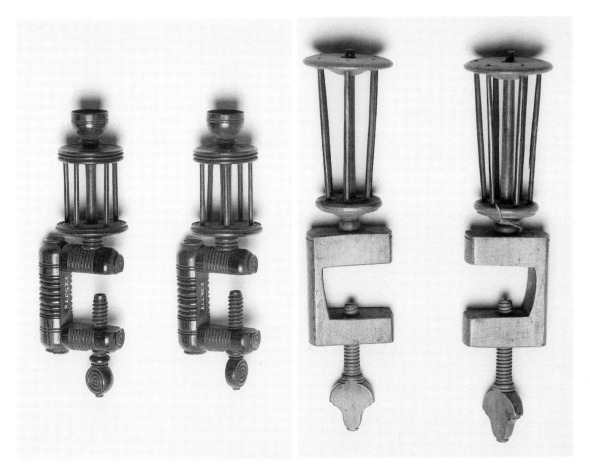

42 *Two pairs of winding clamps. The pair of turned rosewood*
7½ in (19cm) high 1830–50; the larger pair 9 in (22cm), 1860–70,
Gloucester Folk Museum

folded up towards the spindle when not in use. Wooden swifts were
very practical and well-made, but towards the end of the century
free-standing, metal examples, probably imported from America,
were more ornate and less robust. Although after 1840 most threads
were sold ready to use, wool persisted as skeins until recently and
winders were made until the 1950s. A very late design was a cross of
metal wires which revolved on a spindle clamped to a chair in the
style of the earliest examples.

From the late eighteenth until the mid nineteenth century a pair of
winding clamps could be used as an alternative to a single frame.
They were made from wood, bone, ivory, or occasionally metal and
each clamp supported an identical frame (although the finials might
vary) on a spindle with the skein stretched between them. Large
pairs of wooden clamps, up to 12 in (30cm) high, were strong and
practical, but many smaller examples were often too frail for their

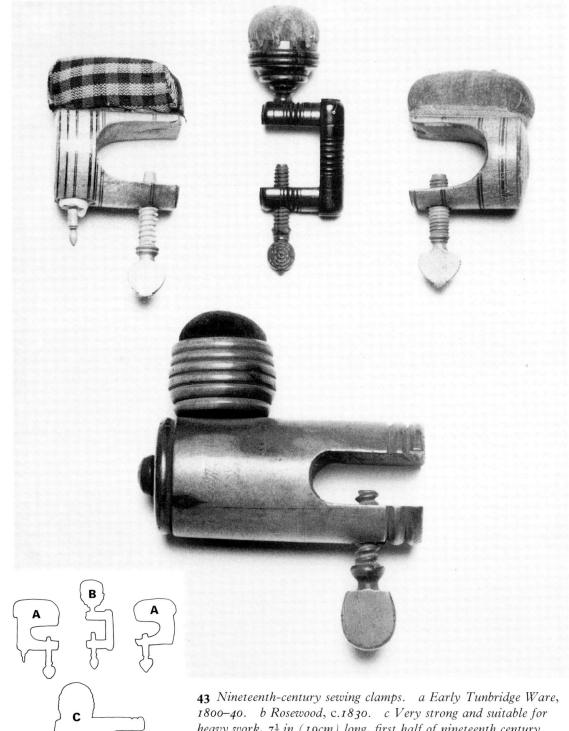

43 *Nineteenth-century sewing clamps. a Early Tunbridge Ware, 1800–40. b Rosewood, c.1830. c Very strong and suitable for heavy work, 7½ in (19cm) long, first half of nineteenth century,* Gloucester Folk Museum

1 *Needle packets.* National Needle Museum, Redditch

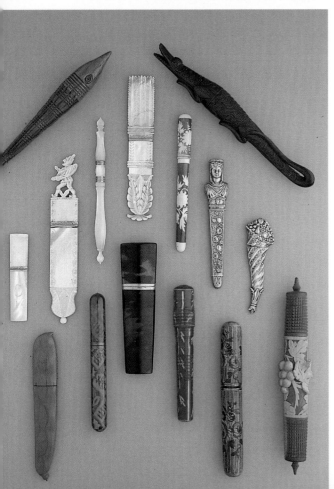

2 *Needle-cases.* (A) *Wood—early nineteenth century* (B) *French glass—1830* (C) *Tortoise-shell—late eighteenth century* (D) *Stained ivory—early nineteenth century* (E) *Painted wood—late eighteenth century* (F) *Carved wood, Swiss/Austrian—late nineteenth century* (G-J) *Mother-of-pearl Palais Royal—1790-1830* (K) *Stained bone, Tyrolean—mid nineteenth century* (L,M) *Silver-gilt, French—early nineteenth century* (N,O) *Wood—late nineteenth century*

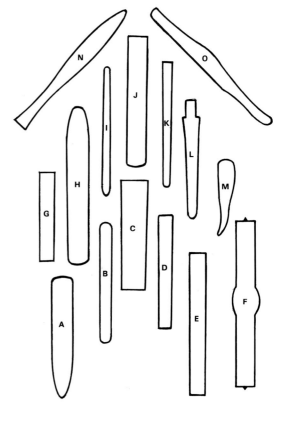

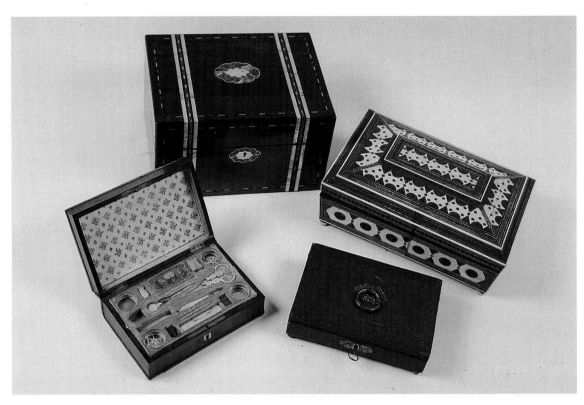

3 *Work boxes, 1810-60,* York Castle Museum

4 *Metal and plaster bobbin stand* c. *1880,* Gloucester Folk Museum

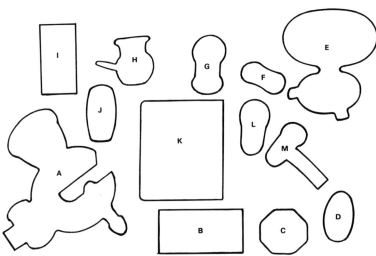

5 *Tunbridge Ware.* (A) *Painted clamp with cottage tape measure* (B) *Mosaic needle book* (C) *Half-Square Mosaic thread winder* (D) *Stick ware pin poppet* (E) *Mosaic pin table* (F) *Stick ware emery* (G) *Stick ware waxer and emery* (H) *Stick ware emery* (I) *Mosaic needle packet holder* (J) *Painted cotton barrel* (K) *Cube pattern needle book* (L) *Stick ware thimble case* (M) *Stick ware tape measure.* Tunbridge Wells Municipal Museum and Art Gallery

6 *Tartan Ware. Knitting ball holder, thread winder, tatting shuttle and sewing cotton box,* York Castle Museum

7 *Scottish Souvenir Ware.* (A,B,C,H,I,J) *Mauchline pincushions, tape measures and needle-case* (D,E,G) *Fernware pincushion, thread box and needle-book* (F) *Box for sewing cottons with coloured print, Clarks* (K) *Black lacquer sewing cotton box with a game 'Pray will you have your fortune told?'*

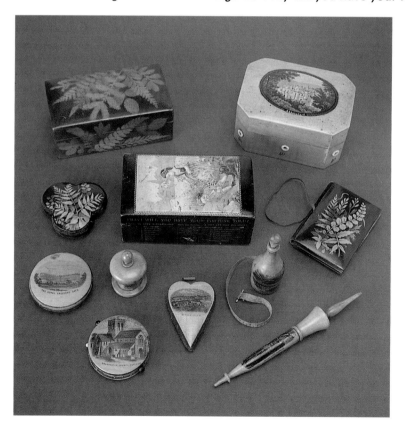

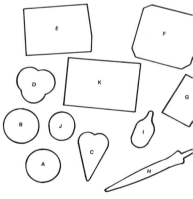

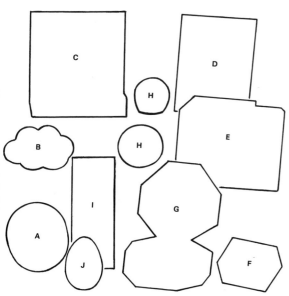

8 *Thread boxes from Coats, Clarks and Chadwicks.* (A) *Anchor Thread Calendar 1878* (B) *Mauchline Ware* (C) *Chadwicks Moravian Crochet cotton, 1930s* (D) *Black lacquer and print* (E) *Mile of Cotton, Empire Exhibition Glasgow, 1938* (F) *'A Friendship Wish'* (G) *Chadwicks' label.* (H) *Crochet or knitting ball holders* (I) *'May Happiness be Ever Thine' game* (J) *Black lacquer and print* Coats Viyella plc

9 *Late nineteenth-century chatelaines,* York Castle Museum

10 *Nineteenth-century pincushions,*
York Castle Museum

11 *Souvenir pin discs and needle book*
with a transfer under glass, 1850-75

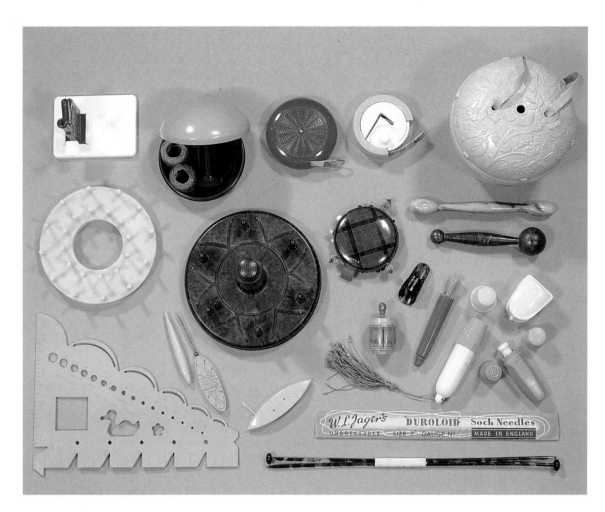

12 *Twentieth-century plastics.* (A) *Multi-purpose free gift* (B) *Woollen flower frame* (C) *Needle threader* (D) *Darning mushroom* (E) *Tape measure* (F) *Knitting wool holder* (G) *Glove darner* (H) *Thimble case* (I) *Thimbles* (J) *Mending kit* (K) *Knitting needles* (L) *Needle-case* (M) *Finger guard* (N) *Tatting shuttle* (O) *Pricker and cover* (P) *Bobbin stand* (Q) *Pin disc*

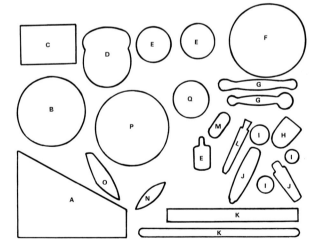

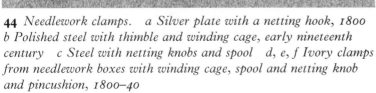

44 *Needlework clamps.   a Silver plate with a netting hook, 1800*
b Polished steel with thimble and winding cage, early nineteenth
century   c Steel with netting knobs and spool   d, e, f Ivory clamps
from needlework boxes with winding cage, spool and netting knob
and pincushion, 1800–40

45 *Hemming bird, late nineteenth century*, Tudor House,
Southampton City Museums

purpose and the screw threads soon stripped. Polished steel clamps were only suitable for fine yarn. Pairs of small bone or ivory clamps were made from 1800–60, but it is unusual to find a matching pair today. Although the majority of winding frames were fixed on to a table with a clamp some rather elegant pieces were made on adjustable, polished wooden stands.

From the latter years of the eighteenth century until the invention of the sewing machine it was common practice to hem with the aid of a hemming clamp; one end of the fabric was fixed to the clamp and held taut in one hand which facilitated working a quick and even stitch with the other. With most materials the work was pinned to the cushion on the top; only very strong fabrics could be held with a stout clamp between the flat jaws and the table (fig 43c). Polished, wooden clamps with a pincushion fixed into a vase-shaped wooden holder may date from the late eighteenth century. Many clamps were made between 1800–40 in painted Tunbridge Ware, either with the familiar bands or a continuous, vermiform line. Those that were gifts or souvenirs also carried a small label with a suitable sentiment. As hemming clamps are rarely found with later Tunbridge styles, it suggests they became unfashionable. Surviving examples show signs of hard wear – they were very useful accessories.

The first lock stitch sewing machine was patented by Elias Howe, an American, in 1846 and made popular a few years later in Britain by Isaac Singer. It relieved the tedious labour of long seams and hems, but ladies of leisure continued to enjoy hand-work of all kinds. When the wooden hemming clamp went out of favour it was replaced by an ingenious gadget – the hemming bird. A popular design in sheet metal was patented in America in 1853 by Charles Waterman, but similar bird-shaped clamps of solid metal were already in use. Fabric was gripped in the bird's beak (they are known as 'grippers' in the USA), and the clamp only served to fix it to a table; by depressing the tail the beak opened and a strong spring held it shut when released. Many hemming birds had a small emery cushion on their backs. Similar birds were made throughout the century. American birds, butterflies, fish, etc. were imported into Britain and others made here, including a gilded brass bird with an emery cushion on a tall, twisted metal stem. Some ornate clamps were made from cast metal, possible after 1870, including a bronze, winged cupid. Although hemming birds or work holders were used over a longer period in the USA than in Britain, a strong, simple, all-metal holder with a velvet pincushion and a spindle for cotton was advertised in *Weldon's Practical Needlework*, *c.*1900, price one shilling, or two with a thimble holder added.

Heavy cushions, on a strong clamp or free-standing, were used to hold the foundation loop for netting. They were weighted with lead shot or a piece of brick and were very practical for artisans. When netting became fashionable in Georgian times, very pretty tools

46 *Hemming butterfly, 1860–80*, Tudor House, Southampton
City Museums

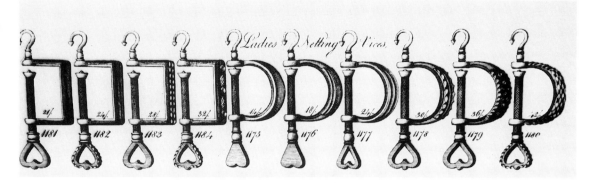

47 *Ladies' netting vices, late eighteenth century,* Tools for the
Trades and Crafts; An eighteenth-century pattern book,
reprinted and edited by R.C. Roberts, 1976

were made with delicate clamps and a pincushion, thread spindle,
netting hook or knob (fig 44a, c and e). These were all fairly small
and usually made of bone or ivory, but from about 1800, or perhaps
even earlier, manufacturers began producing tools for netting from
polished steel. An engraved plate from a trade catalogue is
reproduced in *Tools for the Trades and Crafts* by Kenneth D.
Roberts (fig 47), and shows how the various parts were interchange-
able. The prices were per dozen wholesale. Later netting vices were
made in 'German silver'.

   Another craft which used an accessory clamped to a table was
macramé. The simplest tool was a well-stuffed cushion on one
clamp, but for long lengths of fringe a pair of clamps, with round-
headed or cotton-reel shaped pegs attached to the top, were more
practical; those with 'reels' are easily indentified.

CHAPTER 8

Lacemaking

Lace can be interpreted to include a variety of openwork techniques worked with needles, bobbins, shuttles, hooks, or simply the fingers, to twist, plait or knot the thread. The true laces are needlepoint and bobbin lace, but lacy fabrics can be formed from fine white work, macramé, netting, crochet, tatting or knitting.

Bobbin lace

Bobbin, or pillow, lace is made by twisting and plaiting threads that are wound on bobbins. It was cheaper than needlepoint, and so more commercially viable, but until recently it was not a fashionable craft. A fairly coarse lace using bone bobbins was made in Britain towards the end of the sixteenth century and known as bone lace. Fine quality lace was imported from several European countries, and although a law in 1662 tried to impose a ban to support the home market, it only succeeded in encouraging smuggling. Many skilled Huguenot lace makers fled to Britain after 1685 to escape religious persecution following the Revocation of the Edict of Nantes, and it was their influence that improved the quality of lace making here. Lace making was taught to the poor as a means of earning a living. In 1700 a child of six or seven could earn twenty pence (8p) a week and a hundred years later some men and women were paid twenty-five shillings (£1.25). Various Acts were passed to protect lace makers, but they could not cushion the blow caused by the invention of machines to make net (first patented in 1809 by a Nottingham man) and later lace. When the Window Tax was repealed in 1845, machines made fancy laces to satisfy the new fashion for net curtains. By 1850 earnings had slumped and, in spite of the efforts of several Charities to encourage hand-made lace making, the industry declined and never recovered.

Lace was made in various parts of England, but developed most in two main areas. In the West Country (Devon, Cornwall, Dorset and Somerset) lace making gradually centred on Honiton (pronounced Huniton) in Devon, which gave its name to the local lace. The laces made in Bedfordshire, Buckinghamshire and Northamptonshire, together with parts of Cambridgeshire, Herefordshire, Berkshire and Oxfordshire, were known as East Midlands lace.

The original design for a lace pattern may be dated. The 'draft' was drawn on parchment or card and showed one repeat, pricked holes for the controlling pins and some inked lines to outline the shape. From the draft the lace maker or tradesman made a working parchment on vellum, pasteboard, linen stiffened with shellac, or presspahn (impregnated paper). An East Midlands parchment was up to 14 in (35cm) in length with the pattern, repeated if necessary, along the whole length; all the lines were pricked and some details added in ink. A Honiton parchment showed one complete motif, or 'sprig'. Sometimes the ends of a parchment had short, fabric tabs – 'eches' – to fix it to the pillow. Brass pins were preferred, but they were expensive and some primitive workers used thorns or fishbones. Broken pins could be re-headed with tiny beads or seeds – 'hariffes' (see Chapter 4 and fig 26 h and i). A small pincushion and a pillow on a stand were necessary equipment. Pillows varied in shape but the majority used in the East Midlands were large, fat and cylindrical, while Honiton lace workers preferred a flatter surface. A bobbin winder was a great time-saver and there were various designs; a skein was stretched over a frame and one end of the thread tied to the neck of a bobbin, which was pushed into a holder and, by the action of a fly-wheel, revolved and filled with thread.

Bobbins were between $3\frac{1}{2}$–4 in (88–114mm) long and usually made of bone or hard wood. Dating them is difficult because the decorative designs continued to be used over a long period. The oldest surviving bobbins may be of bone because they were more hard-wearing and outlasted wooden ones of a similar date, but all bobbins in regular use wear out (very thin ones were called 'old maids'). The majority in museums are nineteenth century. Bobbins are still made in wood and plastic; early plastic was in bright colours, while present-day examples are often imitation wood.

Honiton lace was made from separate motifs which were either sewn to a net ground or joined with needle-made bars. The bobbins, or 'lace sticks', were slender and pointed because they had to pass through a loop of thread (fig 48a). Although the practical bobbins used by present-day lacemakers are plain, there is a long tradition of decoration which goes back to the eighteenth century. The designs, usually in red and black, include rings, chequers, flowers, birds, fish, ships, people and mottoes as well as dates and initials.

All East Midlands bobbins (with the exception of some from South Buckinghamshire which were larger and heavier for thicker thread) had a ring of beads attached to the bottom end to keep them steady on the pillow and help with identification – a wide flounce needed several hundred bobbins. The beads were threaded on copper wire and known as the 'spangle' or 'jingle'. The centre bead was larger or different from the rest and was sometimes replaced with a button or shell for luck. The smaller beads, of random colour, might include some hand-made 'square cuts', cut from a rod of softened glass and squeezed with two files to give a textured surface; pink and clear glass were more common than amber or turquoise. A

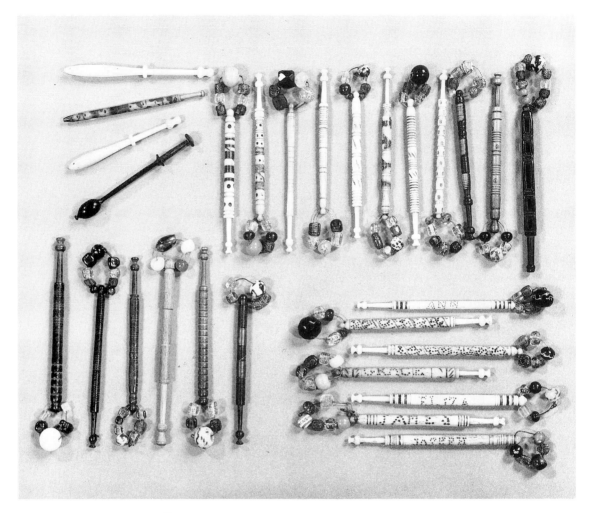

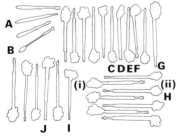

48 *Pillow lace bobbins.   a Stained wood, Honiton*
b Polished wood, Flemish. All other bobbins from the East Midlands
c Pewter inlay 'butterfly' on bone   d Turned and stained 'tiger' on
bone   e Turned, drilled and stained 'leopard' on bone   f Wood
inlay 'bitted'   g Wood 'mother and babe' or 'church window'
h Turned bone with names added (i) I LIKE MY LOVE TOO MUCH TO
CHANGE. *(ii)* WHEN THIS YOU SEE REMEMBER ME   *i Polished wood*
and brass wire   j A twentieth-century bobbin (all the others are
probably nineteeth century)

'bird cage' was made from a large bead surrounded by tiny ones
threaded on wire.

Some bobbins were carved as special gifts for a mother, sister or
sweetheart, but these were never common. A 'cow-in-calf' or 'jack-
in-the-box' pulled apart to reveal a small bobbin inside the shank. A
'church window' or 'mother-and-babe' had a tiny bobbin carved

within an aperture in the shank. Decorations on bobbins were not regional (fig 48 g).

Most bobbins were turned on a lathe and sold by pedlars at the door or hucksters at the fair. Some of them were personalized by the addition of names or messages which could be added by the purchaser, but were usually done by the maker during manufacture or to order while you waited. Small holes were drilled, or burned with a hot wire, and filled with paint or coloured wax. Most of them had a single name, but longer sentiments could be spiralled round the shank: e.g. 'I LIKE MY LOVE TOO MUCH TO CHANGE' (fig 48h). Bobbins could be inscribed for Sunday School prizes, political parties, royal events, battles and even public hangings. Turned bobbins could be decorated in other ways, for example with bands of brass wire or rings of pewter, or pewter could be inlaid as spots for 'leopards', bands for 'tigers' or with a curious arrowhead to represent a 'butterfly' (fig 48e, d and c). Dark wood could be inlaid with light to make a 'bitted' bobbin, (fig 48f), or bobbins could be stained with various colours. As there are so many different forms of decoration, visits to museums in lacemaking districts are recommended for further study.

Macramé

Macramé is one of the oldest types of lace and a precursor of bobbin lace. In early times weavers were reluctant to waste the yarn at the beginning and end of a piece of fabric, and they found that by twisting and knotting it with their fingers it could be made into a decorative border on towels, shawls and mats. In the Near East this developed into a craft making entire strips; vertical threads were tied to a horizontal thread stretched across an oblong pillow and then plaited with the fingers. In sixteenth-century Europe it was known as *punto à groppo*, a name later replaced by *macramé*, from the Turkish word for towel. It was very popular in Britain during the eighteenth and nineteenth centuries and has recently been revived.

No tools were necessary. In the late nineteenth century strong thread was sold in boxes by Barbour, Strutt and others. Barbour also advertised a special frame to hold the work which consisted of a long padded pillow clamped to a table, similar to the Anyon 'Loom and Patent Tension Frame'. Pairs of clamps, with spools to hold the horizontal thread, are described in Chapter 7.

If fairly coarse, light-coloured twine was used, macramé could be worked by candlelight. This was important as, with very few exceptions, no fine needlework could be done after dark until electric light was available.

Teneriffe lace

Spanish lace, including Sun lace or *Sols*, is a type of embroidery on radiating threads sewn into a circular hole in a piece of fabric. It was exported to Spanish colonies in Central and South America and the Canary Islands, where the local inhabitants adapted the pattern for their own use. One type, where individual motifs were joined to make a very delicate fabric, became known as Spanish Wheel or Teneriffe lace. This found its way to Britain in the nineteenth century.

Originally, Teneriffe lace was worked on a piece of parchment on which was drawn a small circle with many radiants. Each radiant was pricked at the point where it met the circumference and a single line of running stitches, in and out of these holes, gave the foundation for thread radiants, sewn using a netting needle.

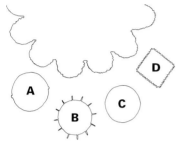

49 *Teneriffe lace tablets with doily, c.1900.   a Vicar's Teneriffe Wheel, c.1900   b Daisy Wheel, c.1960   c Briggs Patent Teneriffe Wheel, c.1890   d Dryad Teneriffe Frame, c.1930*

Subsequently, embroidered patterns were worked on these with a sewing needle and thread. The introduction of a lace tablet, towards the end of the century, simplified and popularized the craft. The earliest tablets were made of ivory or bone with a notched edge but cheap card discs largely replaced them about 1890. They were made in various sizes by several firms including Morris and Yeoman (patented) and Vicars, who had identical designs. The 2 in (50mm) tablet was made from two pieces of card glued together and covered with waxed paper or cloth, on which was printed a working pattern; forty-six black-headed and two white-headed pins were stuck into the edge. William Briggs' brass wheels, with concentric circles of small holes to hold pins, may also date from the 1890s, their celluloid examples from after 1900. During the 1930s Dryad produced a range of metal tablets with saw-tooth edges in circles, elipses, squares, rectangles and triangles which could be folded to release the motif; about 1960 a 'Daisy' wheel had retractable radiants for the same purpose. The *Anchor Manual of Needlework* (1958) gave instructions for making Teneriffe lace with a folding metal tablet with a saw-toothed edge and by the earlier method of pricked holes on a card.

CHAPTER 9

Netting

Netting developed simultaneously in several countries as a most useful craft and the simple tools have changed little throughout history – these consist of a netting needle, or shuttle, to hold the thread and a gauge to keep the mesh of constant size. They produce a hard-wearing fabric, in which each stitch is independent with no chance of unravelling, which has always been invaluable to farmers, fisherman, hunters and domestic users.

Some netting needles in museums are thought to be 3000 years old; certainly netting is frequently mentioned in the Bible and some figures depicted on Egyptian monuments are clearly wearing netted garments. The use of plain netting as a basis for embroidered patterns was probably introduced into Europe from the Middle East during the twelfth century, a hundred years later fine, white network was developed for ecclesiastical purposes. It had the appearance of lace and was called *lacis* or *filet* (from the French). Netting became fashionable in sixteenth-century Britain, and by the eighteenth century wealthy Georgian ladies owned beautiful netting tools which they kept in decorative boxes. Netting continued to be popular into the early nineteenth century for making little silk purses but then went out of favour, to be superseded by crochet and other crafts that were more portable. However, practical nets were still made by ladies for their homes and gardens, and so the craft survived.

Most netting needles were made of steel, wood, bone or ivory, and tortoise-shell was occasionally used before 1800. Steel needles were necessary for the finest work; bone and ivory could be used in various sizes, but wood was not suitable for the smallest tools. The simple shape, open at both ends, had a small hole below one fork to secure the thread which was wound around the needle (fig 50 a, c and d). Bone and wooden needles were also made in an alternative shape where the thread was wound around a spike (fig 50b). Needles varied in length between 3–10 in (7–25cm). One draper's catalogue in 1903 mentions only steel needles, but in 1931 another wholesaler had steel, wood and bone needles and meshes of wood or bone.

Netting meshes, mesh-sticks or spools, were made of similar materials to the needles. The circumference of a mesh-stick creates a mesh twice is own size, and needle and mesh have to be compatible with the type of thread. Most meshes were round and pointed at

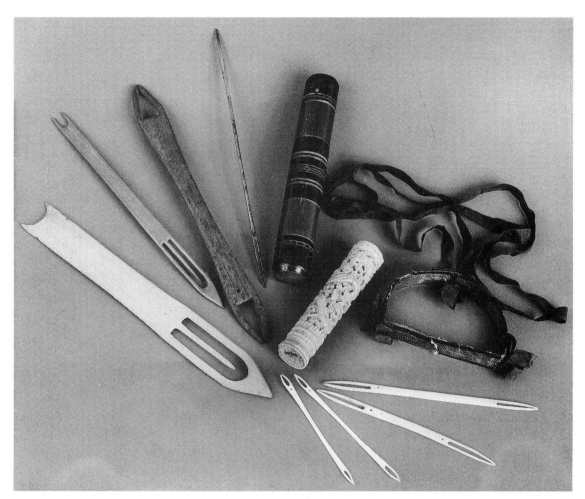

50 *Netting tools.   a Bone netting needles, early to mid nineteenth century   b, d Wooden and steel needles, nineteenth or early twentieth century   c Crude, home-made needle   e, f Wooden and ivory cases which could hold netting needles, first half nineteenth century   g Netting stirrup of braid-covered metal, first half nineteenth century, York Castle Museum*

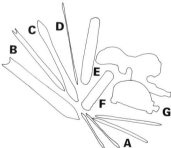

each end, and after 1850 some were numbered to correspond with knitting needles, which they resembled; sometimes it is very difficult to differentiate between round netting meshes and knitting needles. Flat meshes of wood or bone, with rounded ends, could be used for net but were essential for fringes; they were made in various widths from ½ in (12mm) upwards. Similar flat tools of ivory, bone or plastic are used by printers and book-binders for folding paper and may be mistaken for meshes, but printers' 'bones' are usually stouter to withstand heavier wear.

When netting it is essential to hold the foundation loop taut.

Almost anything will suffice – such as a hook fixed to a wall or a chairback – but many workers preferred something more portable which could be simply practical or a decorative object. Some netters pinned the foundation loop to a very heavy, large cushion covered with strong cloth; these were either free-standing or attached to a clamp. An alternative method was to hold the loop with the foot, which was easier if a stirrup was used. Most stirrups, (the word describes the shape exactly) were quite crude, made from a piece of hard wood about 4 in (10cm) in length and $1\frac{1}{2}$ in (38mm) wide, with a hole bored in each end. Ribbon or tape, of sufficient length to reach from the floor to the worker's knee and back, was threaded through the holes and sewn together under the wood. More ornamental stirrups were made with embroidered ribbons or metal shapes could be purchased and the ribbon added (fig 50g). The latter were similar to spool knaves, but it is usually possible to distinguish them as netting stirrups were made from very plain, base metal and if they have a cord or ribbon attached this must be of sufficient length to be suitable for its purpose. To give a more elegant tool for finer and more delicate work, the Georgians used a small knob or hook attached to a sewing or winding clamp. Examples in ivory or bone were sometimes included in the fittings of a work box. From about 1800 polished steel netting vices were made for this specific purpose (figs 44 a, c, e and 47).

Containers to store netting tools were often more decorative than the basic implements. A few small netting boxes were made in the latter half of the eighteenth century. They held the needles and meshes and included a small roller with a slit or hole for the foundation loop. The roller was fitted with a ratchet and, by turning a handle, the worked net could be stored on it. Netting rollers were included in some work boxes and tables from 1800–30. Neither of these were in common use. Many more tools were kept in decorative cylinders, similar to but larger than needlecases, they are not easy to identify unless the tools and cases match exactly and it is unwise to be dogmatic. Fine quality, large (over 6 in/15cm) cases, made of carved ivory or tortoise-shell, filigree or enamelled metal or straw work, could be Georgian netting cases, but less expensive examples of a similar size may be for Victorian crochet hooks. Smaller, cylindrical cases were used for short netting or crochet tools and also for bodkins.

CHAPTER 10

Tambour work and crochet

Tambouring

Chain stitch embroidery can be worked with a needle and thread, but an almost indistinguishable stitch may be done more quickly with a tambour hook. Tambour work originated in China and India, where it is still practised, and was introduced into Europe about 1760. It soon became a fashionable craft in Britain and in 1772 a visitor to Blickling Hall, Norfolk, remarked that he had seen the ladies doing their tambour work.

A tambour hook is similar to a crochet hook, but more pointed to enable it to be pushed easily through fabric. The actual hook was always made of steel and for everyday tools it was fixed into a plain, bone handle, but expensive tambour hooks had beautiful handles and covers made from carved bone or ivory, mother-of-pearl, silver or polished agate. These usually had four to six hooks, in graded sizes, stored inside the handle and the chosen hook was held in place with a thumb screw. All hooks with a thumb screw are tambour hooks, but a single hook permanently fixed in a handle may be mistaken for a crochet tool – it is important to examine the shape of the hook. Very few decorative hooks were made after 1840.

Before commencing the work a design was drawn or printed on muslin or silk. Patterns to copy were available. The fabric was stretched over a frame, either a small round one or, for larger pieces of work, a rectangular slate or tent frame. A tambour was a French drum and old frames resembled them in shape; subsequently all round frames made from two hoops were known as tambour frames. Embroidery frames were often sold by itinerant traders who carried them around the countryside on their backs. Stitches were made by passing the hook through the fabric and back, catching a thread running underneath and thus forming a chain. To guide the thread there were special thimbles, made from a sheet of metal, usually brass, rolled up but open at the top like a tailor's thimble and with a little notch on one side in which the needle was laid. They were worn on the forefinger of the right hand but may not have been in common use as very few have surivived, in spite of still being recommended at the end of the nineteenth century in Thérèse de Dillmont's *Encyclopedia of Needlework*.

Tambour work required a continuous thread and some workers

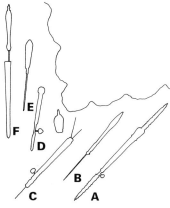

51 *Tambour hooks and muslin shawl with tambour work, c.1800. a Ivory, late eighteenth century   b Agate handle with single hook, mid nineteenth century   c Bone, early to mid nineteenth century d Impractical mother-of-pearl, probably from a work box, early nineteenth century   e Plain hook, c.1850   f Ivory handle, red leather case, early to mid nineteenth century*

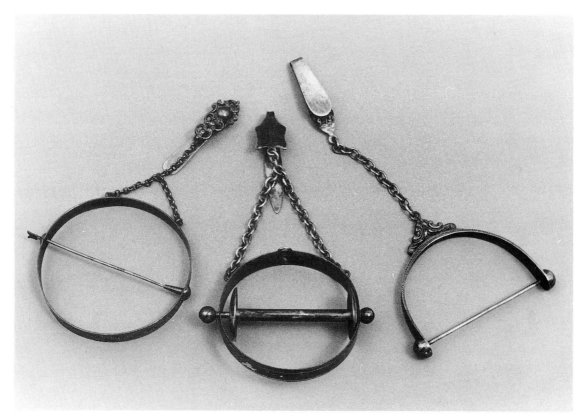

52 *Spool knaves, 1880–1910, probably used to hold crochet cotton,* York Castle Museum

drew this directly from a revolving skein winder. A special device to hold the thread was called a spool knave or reel holder. It consisted of a spindle fixed into a semi-circle or complete ring of metal, bone or ivory and suspended from the waistband by a hook on a short chain. Eighteenth-century spool knaves were fine quality ivory or silver with a drum-shaped spindle to hold the thread, but after 1800 the drum was replaced by a bar screwed into position. After 1830 most of them were intended for crochet thread, and towards the end of the century a bracelet was preferred to a hook and the spindle held with a spring. A few were made of silver or silver-plate after 1900 and some cheaper, patented gadgets were sold (fig 55a). A plastic spool knave was recently given away with copies of a woman's magazine.

Tambour work was also a cottage industry and thrived in Scotland from 1780–1820, but when a machine was invented to embroider muslin the art was not viable. However plain, functional hooks were re-introduced commercially about 1860 for beadwork and these continued to be used on top-quality fashions.

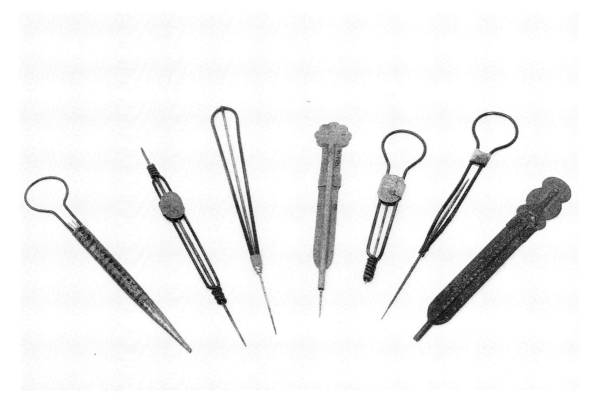

54 *Metal crochet tools with retractable or pivotted hooks,*
advertised 1895–1905, York Castle Museum

Crochet

Crochet, worked with a round-ended hook, was known in sixteenth-century Europe and practised by nuns in Ireland before it spread to other parts of Britain during the eighteenth century, when it was known as 'shepherd's crook knitting'. *Crochet* is a French word meaning a small hook and the earliest reference to this name was in the mid-1830s when the first instruction books were published. It became very popular and pattern books proliferated after 1840.

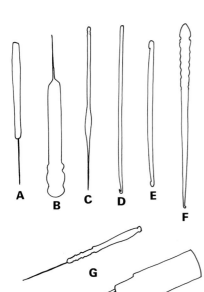

All crochet hooks were practical tools, even if they were decorated. Eighteenth-century hooks made of wood or bone are difficult to identify, but they are all large because wool was the only material worked until fine thread and fine steel hooks were introduced about 1820. The Victorians used hooks of steel, wood, bone, ivory , vulcanite, gutta-percha (a whitish, rubber-like substance, 1845–1930) and, from the 1890s, celluloid. A few mother-of-pearl hooks were made, but they were not of much use. Steel hooks combined with another material for the handle and all-bone were the most common. The most decorative were made from ivory, probably pre-1870. Some particularly delightful hooks were made,

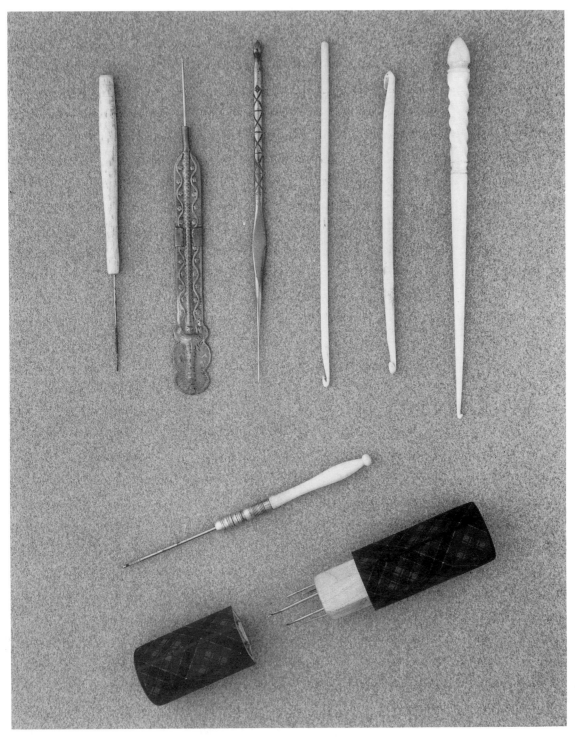

53 *Crochet hooks.   a Bone handle with brass stud, 1900*
b Metal 'Lighthouse' with retractable hook, 1900   c Blued steel,
1900 d, e Bone   f Impractical mother-of-pearl, c.1830   g Tartan
Ware set of six hooks with one bone handle, c.1850

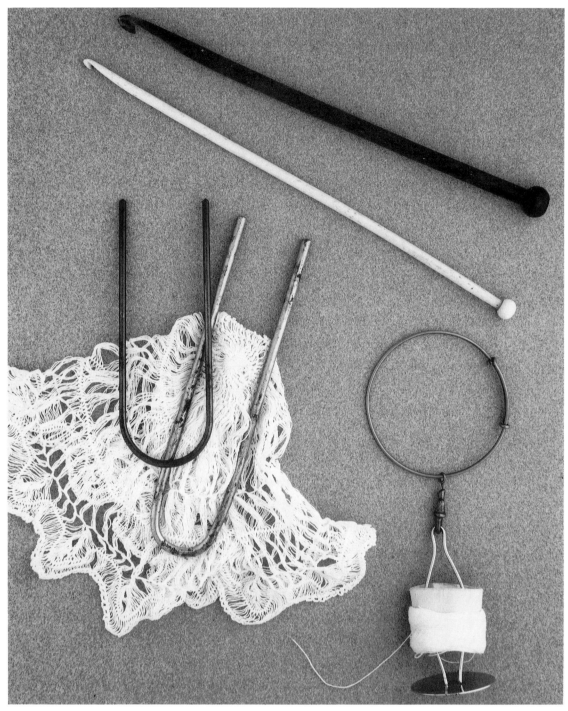

55 *Crochet tools.   a 'The Ownlee' holder for crochet cotton with bracelet, 1910   b Late nineteenth-century tools for hairpin crochet and doily   c Tricot crochet hooks, bone, second half of nineteenth century, tortoiseshell celluloid, 1880–1920*

the majority with turned patterns and a few delicately carved animals, birds and figures. Sets of hooks in graded sizes were sold in fancy boxes of card or wood, in which the chosen hook was always secured by a screw or collet, never by a thumb screw. In 1886 Lewis, Wright and Bayliss sold steel hooks at seventeen shillings (85p) a gross, all bone and wooden hooks to retail at a penny each and vulcanite for a half-penny. At about the same time several firms sold a selection of ingenious but impractical flat hooks with retractable or pivoted heads. These had such names as 'Magic', 'Surprise' and 'Favourite', but were only manufactured for about 20 years. In Rotherham's wholesale catalogue, 1905, there is an assortment of bone hooks, either plain or simply-turned, and several steel hooks with bone handles, including one with a metal ring at the end and another with a brass stud. The steel hooks were either plain or pivoted, and the retractable version was no longer made. Wholesale prices varied from plain bone at three shillings and threepence a gross – about a farthing each – to a fairly plain but stout, steel hook at eight shillings for the same number.

Several interesting advertisements for needlework tools and accessories were included in editions of *Weldon's Crochet* and in other booklets in their *Practical Needlework* series. About 1920 'Stratnoid' crochet hooks were described as 'rustless under all conditions', which was not surprising as the material used by Strattons for a variety of tools was celluloid. Also in the advertisement was a table for comparing the new Stratnoid standard sizes with the old equivalents; the standard was the accepted gauge for wire, but the 'old' numbering of 2, 3, 4, $4\frac{1}{2}$, 5, $5\frac{1}{2}$, etc. would make it very difficult to work from old patterns today.

Tunisian crochet

Stout hooks of bone or wood up to 20 in (50cm) in length with a knob at one end were used for Tunisian or Tricot crochet (fig 55c). About 1860 this was claimed as a new invention, but it had older origins. Whole rows of loops were kept on the hook and worked off on the next row, so it was only suitable for straight work where strips could be joined together for the required width, for example on counterpanes. Very few instructions were published, but some were included in Caulfield and Saward's *The Dictionary of Needlework*, 1882. Tricot hooks, named after the basic stitch, were not listed in general drapery catalogues after 1920, but there has been a recent rivival and a few metal hooks have been made since 1960.

Hairpin crochet

Hairpin crochet, also known as fork work, required a two-pronged tool and a crochet hook to make a lacy fabric for doilies, shawls, collars, etc. It was very popular throughout the second half of the

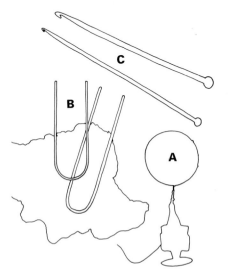

nineteenth century and instructions were included in some books until 1940, although it is doubtful if the tools could be purchased at this date.

Early forks, which they resembled, were made of wood, bone or ivory with a slim handle to facilitate rotating the work as it progressed. After 1880 forks were replaced by a U-shaped metal tool made from firm wire or a thicker rod, between $3\frac{1}{2}$–7 in (88–117mm) in length (fig 55b). It was possible to use ordinary, large hairpins but they were too short to produce even work. An alternative tool was made in France (and Britain?) from two steel knitting needles joined by a sliding bar of varied widths. About 1900 *Weldon's Practical Needlecraft* called the work 'Krotchee Crochet' which used a 'Krotchee hairpin or fork' but in their *Encyclopedia of Needlework*, 1930 and reprinted in the 1940s, the name had reverted to hairpin crochet and an illustration showed two forks (bone or wood), three steel and one bone hairpin. To make a fringe in hairpin crochet, a wooden fringing fork was used with one narrow and three or four wider prongs.

CHAPTER 11
Knotting and tatting

Knotting

Knotting home-spun linen thread was known in late-medieval Britain and was widespread by the seventeenth century. Through-

56 *Knotting shuttles*, left *painted papier mâché, 1790,* right *tortoise-shell, 1800, and a ball of knotted thread,* York Castle Museum

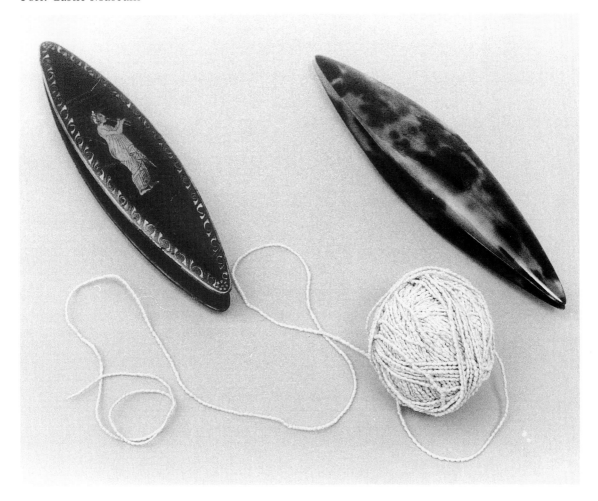

out the eighteenth century it was a very fashionable pastime, but it declined quickly after 1800. Thread was wound on a shuttle and by a series of identical knots a continuous length of beaded cord was produced, which was then couched down on costume or furnishings for decoration. In Cotehele House, Cornwall, there is a rare set of chairs with eighteenth-century loose covers decorated with knotting. It was extremely simple and required little thought, which made it an ideal occupation in company. Yards and yards of cord, together with the shuttle and thread, were kept in pretty little bags made for the purpose.

Knotting shuttles were 4–6 in (10–15cm) in length and 1–2 in (25–50mm) wide. They were made from two oval blades, rounded at both ends and joined in the middle. The tips of the blades did not touch, if a shuttle has a very wide gap this may indicate that it predates the manufacture of fine linen thread in the eighteenth century. Knotting was enjoyed by the wealthy classes who could afford fine quality shuttles; tortoise-shell, very light to use, and ivory, very smooth to handle, were most common but they were also made of gold, silver, enamel, mother-of-pearl, papier mâché, horn and decorated wood. The most ornate shuttles were French. When the craft declined, many of these beautiful objects were treasured in display cabinets and have survived in fine condition. The plain, wooden shuttle (fig 57a) is unusual, but it clearly shows the difference between a round-ended knotting shuttle and the more pointed tatting tool.

Tatting

Tatting (a nineteenth-century word of unknown origin) came from the East, where the work was called by their word for a shuttle and arrived in Europe in the sixteenth century. During the eighteenth century it was known as *frivolité* in France, and may have been worked in Britain at this time, but it did not receive much attention until the decline of knotting. Tatting was very popular during the second half of the nineteenth century and, although less fashionable after 1920, it was worked and shuttles have been made to the present day.

At the beginning of the nineteenth century tatting was a succession of knots over a loop of its own thread drawn up to form an entire oval, which was tied to other ovals to make a delicate but strong lace. Later the ovals were assembled with crochet and in 1860 a method was discovered to join the motifs while working. Tatting was a simple craft once the basic technique was mastered.

Tatting shuttles were smaller than those for knotting, being no more than 3 in (75mm) long and $\frac{3}{4}$ in (19mm) wide, but of similar design except that the tips of the blades were pointed and almost touched – they had to be sufficiently close to prevent the thread escaping freely. After 1870 a new technique required a pair of

57 *Tatting shuttles and a doily.   a Plain wooden knotting*
shuttle for comparison   b Ivory with steel studding, early
nineteenth century   c, d Tartan Ware   e, f, i Carved ivory,
mid nineteenth century   h, g Bone was used until the 1930s
j Mother-of-pearl   k Hook and ring, 1860–1900
l Polished wood   m Papier mâché inlaid with abalone shell,
second half nineteenth century   n Tortoise-shell, 1820–30,
Tudor House, Southampton City Museums

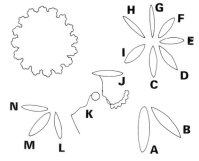

shuttles, and in the late 1890s a shuttle with a small hook at one end
was introduced. Tatting was worked by a wider circle of ladies than
knotting and, although some could afford expensive shuttles, the
majority of nineteenth-century tools were bone, supplemented by
various souvenir wares. Since 1900 shuttles have been made from
bone, vulcanite or celluloid, and from the 1950s, thermoplastic.

A purling pin, similar to a large common pin or a hairpin, was used
after 1860 as a gauge when working purls, or picots, around the
outside edges. Towards the end of the century a small hook was sold
to pull the connecting loops through as the work progressed. It was

attached by a short chain to a metal or bone ring which was placed over a thumb or finger, but many workers considered it unnecessary and found a steel crochet hook more effective. They were sometimes fitted into needlework sets, but were not included in wholesalers' catalogues. Most were probably sold by mail order through advertisments in magazines (fig 57k).

CHAPTER 12

Knitting

Knitting may have originated in Egypt or Arabia, but from fragments that have survived it seems probable that the stocking stitch used there was made with a threaded needle. By 500 AD Arabs were expert knitters on a knitting frame and it is thought that this craft spread across Europe from the Mediterranean.

Frame knitting was also known as peg, row or ring knitting; the work was attached to the pegs and descended through the centre of the frame as it progressed to form a tube of fabric. It was used to make cords, purses, bags, caps, stockings and other garments in the round, the size of the work varying with the diameter of the frame. Small frames were used to make cords, and are still popular with children who can improvize with a wooden cotton reel and a few nails, unless they have a 'Knitting Nancy' (an old term) shaped like a simple doll. It is sometimes called French knitting, which may have a connection with the medieval guilds of French stocking knitters.

Until the latter part of the nineteenth century small purses were made at home for all members of the family. Various techniques were used including knitting, netting and later, crochet. A peg-knitting frame was adapted to make purses (fig 58d) and known as a *Moule Turc* or a purse mould, but this name was misleading as it was also used for another tool (fig 58e). Purse-moulds were thimble-shaped and made from wood, or occasionally ivory, with two rows of holes in shallow grooves near the rim. A silk thread was wound around the grooves, secured by temporary stitches through the holes, and a purse worked from these on the outside of the mould in buttonhole stitch, or *à feston*. Very few thimble-moulds were made after 1800 when miser, or stocking purses, became fashionable.

The earliest miser purses were made from netting sewn into a tube with a long slit in the centre. Two loose rings were kept on the purse by 'jingles', suitable decorative items sewn to each end. Later, knitting and crochet replaced netting. Some purses were formed over a flat, wooden mould, or they could be stretched into shape on a purse stretcher. This was made from two pieces of wood which formed a cylinder when placed together; tension was applied to the purse by forcing the two pieces apart by means of a thumb screw at each end.

Beadwork was a popular pastime and many purses were decorated with beads. Fine beads were imported from Venice and Bohemia in

58 *Knitting frames.   a Knitting ring, late nineteenth century*
b 'French knitting' tube, ivory, early nineteenth century
c Wooden 'french knitting' tube   d Moule Turc *purse mould,*
probably eighteenth century   e Purse mould and purse worked
with beads à feston, *early nineteenth century*

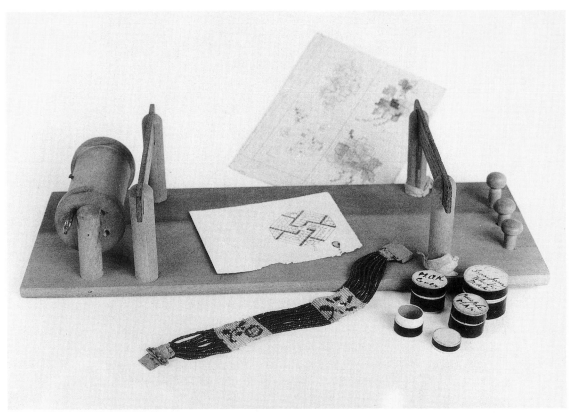

59 *Apache Bead Loom patented 1903, pill boxes of beads,*
hand-made patterns and a beaded bracelet made on a loom,
York Castle Museum

the late eighteenth century, but they were expensive. Cheaper beads made in France and Britain were bought by the Victorians from a haberdasher or pedlar. Small beads were sold by weight, 'pound beads', or threaded on to cotton in bunches, 12 rows per 1 bunch. A few ladies had special boxes to store their beads; there is a magnificent one in The Museum of Costume, Bath, dated 1800–10, containing many small circular and rectangular boxes with a different painting on each lid. Most beads were stored in anything that was suitable and old pill boxes were frequently used, decorated with printed paper and labelled with the type and colour of beads inside. Although small table looms for weaving braids were used throughout the eighteenth century and continued until the 1820s, there is scant evidence of looms for beadwork until the end of the century. In 1903 The Apache Loom was patented by H.A. Austin in Boston, Massachusetts; fig 59, in York Castle Museum, has a bill in the box for 'Beads 3½d, postage 1d'.

Hand knitting using knitting needles was introduced into Britain for caps in about 1450, and the first knitted stockings were made

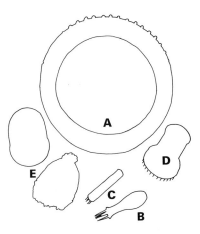

fifty years later. By the middle of the sixteenth century hand knitting had became an important source of income for working men and women in England, and it spread to Scotland and Wales during the early 1600s. Knitting could be worked while occupied with other tasks and as late as 1900 lead miners in North-East England, who lived on site, earned a little extra money on the walk to and from home each weekend. Knitting became a fashionable pastime during the eighteenth century.

The first knitting schools for the poor were established during the sixteenth century, but until 1780 they rarely taught reading and writing, which developed after 1784 with the spread of Sunday Schools. By 1864 all children could have part-time education and when School Boards were established under the 1870 Education Act, knitting became compulsory for girls.

The oldest surviving knitting pattern is dated 1655 but it is a rarity, as most knitters carried instructions in their head. One of the first pattern books in the last century was published in the 1830s, intended to meet the needs of teachers in National Schools which had been founded in the 1790s by The National Society for Promoting Education of the Poor.

The first pattern book for the general public was probably a slim volume by Jane Gaugin in 1837, followed three years later by her *Lady's Assistant*. Miss Gaugin claimed to have invented abbreviations and gave a key for the symbols: B = backstitch (purl), T = take-in (decrease), P = plain stitch, L = purl two together and O = open – bring the thread in front and pass it over. They were not universally adopted, but several years later the series *Royal Magazine of Knitting, Netting and Crochet*, price one penny, used similar symbols without a key and with many errors. Eventually, in June 1849, a letter from the Editress admitted she had received so many complaints, 'All the previous numbers will be re-printed with corrections and in future I will test the receipts [patterns] before insertion'.

In 1850 Marie Cooper wrote *The New Guide to Knitting and Crochet* and hoped it would be instructive and amusing. She assured her readers that she was practically acquainted with these arts and warranted them correct. Unfortunately, in common with many publications of this period, some patterns omitted the size of needles, the quantity or type of yarn and there were no illustrations. Her 'receipts' must be some of the briefest in print:

Directions for a Full-Sized Quilt
No. 18 cotton No. 20 pins
Eight stripes with 113 stitches each with a border of
50 stitches. A counterpane without a border will require
more stripes.

Several publishers offered prizes to subscribers for original patterns, but not all the contributors were honest. A Miss J. Adams sent

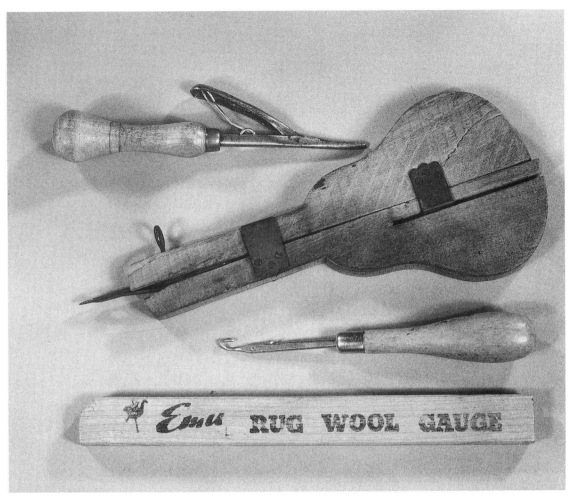

60 *Rug making tools. a Tool for making a rag rug, 1920–50*
b The 'Home Rug Making Machine', 1900   c Latchet hook for
knotted rugs, 1930 onwards   d Rug wool gauge, 1950

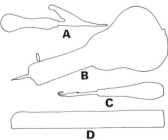

a design for a collar to *Knitting for the Million* in 1849 and, obviously
pleased with her reward, subsequently had it published the
following year in *The Parisian Knitted Collar Book*.

Fortunately some patterns were both reliable and practical,
including those from Ackermann's of The Strand in the 1840s, Mlle
Riego de la Branchardière's books (in English) from 1846–88, and
Mrs Beeton, who edited magazines in the 1850s, but pride of place
must go to Mrs Weldon and Thérèse de Dillmont. Mrs Weldon
started *The Ladies Journal* in 1879 and introduced the popular series
of *Weldon's Practical Needlework* in 1886 which was published
monthly for many years. It was in a volume issued in 1906 that the
present system of knitting abbreviations was first published.

Thérèse de Dillmont wrote her *Encyclopedia of Needlework* in the early 1880s; it is still in print and used as a practical book today.

The first knitting leaflet was probably sold in 1899 by John Paton, who merged with Baldwin in 1920. James Baldwin of Halifax had begun manufacturing knitting yarns in the 1790s and in 1807 he invented a system for numbering shades, some of which are still used. Baldwin also increased his range of wools to include a thick, worsted 'Turkey wool', suitable for rugs. Cottagers made peggy mats, or rag rugs, from old clothing cut into strips and looped into sacks with a large hook, or later a tool with a spring grip (fig 60a). In 1930 rug hooks cost 4½d each. Turkey wool was cut into short lengths and knotted with a latched hook into burlap, a coarse fabric of jute or hemp (later canvas was preferred) to imitate the craft of the carpet weaver (fig 60a). Various gadgets for rug making were less successful, for example 'The Home Rug Making Machine', *c.*1900, price one shilling and threepence, was used on burlap or flannel stretched over a square frame; a continuous length of wool was threaded into the needle and pushed through the fabric forming a loop on the underside.

Knitting wools were a sideline in Victorian drapers and Berlin Wool Repositories. The first specialist shops opened in the 1880s but were rare until 1900.

The method of using a draw plate to reduce wire to a fine gauge for knitting needles was first used in Germany. Bone and wood were used to knit coarser, home-spun wool. The name needle, pin, wire or prick is arbitrary and regional; no term implies the presence of a knob, which first appeared in 1835. The majority of needles are very difficult to date but it may be helpful to consider fashions in knitting. Very fine steel needles were used commercially in the late seventeenth century to make fashionable gloves, but they may have been imported and it is unlikely that any have survived. Fine needles were made in Britain during the eighteenth century for ladies to knit small trifles in silk. The smallest were 24 gauge wire (0.022 in/0.56mm), and size 20 were still made by Milwards in 1930. Until the end of the nineteenth century most people who knitted for a living used fairly blunt needles because they were suitable for their method of working – the loop was placed on the right-hand needle rather than the right-hand needle inserted into the loop. It was very quick, but required the use of a knitting sheath to support the right-hand needle – this is discussed later. The Victorians had a wide choice of needles – steel, ivory, bone, whalebone, rosewood, ebony, cane and plastic (celluloid under various trade names) from 1880. Blued steel was used until 1925 and nickel-plated steel after 1900. Abel Morrall called their product 'Aero', a name they retained for anodised aluminium in 'various shades' in 1930. Today the majority of metal needles are in only grey or white.

Until 1840 needles were rarely sold in numbered sizes, although steel was determined by the gauge of the wire; it varied between

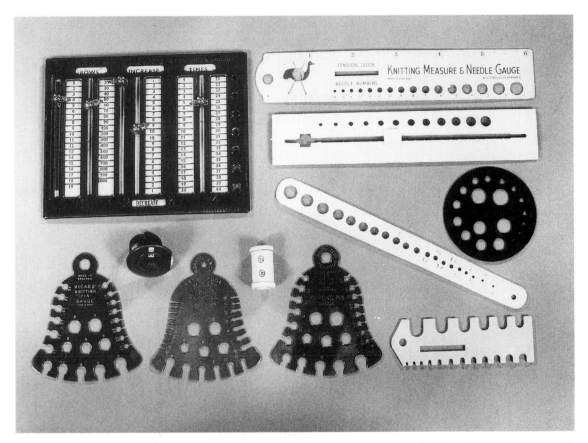

61 *Knitting needle gauges and row counters.   a 'Bell' gauge, gilt brass, patented 1847   b Vicars and Woodfield, plated metal, 1900–30   c Green painted metal, 1930s   d, e, f Plastic needle and tension gauges, 1940–60   g Ivory with metric sizes, mid nineteenth century   h Bronzed metal multi-purpose accessory, 1920–30 i Row counter, metal with plastic clip, 1920–30   j Plastic row counter, 1950*

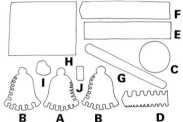

countries and was not standardized. Miss Lambert (who wrote two popular books of knitting patterns in 1843 and 1845) is credited with inventing a disc-shaped needle gauge with sizes 1–26. The famous 'Bell-gauge', in gilt brass, was patented in 1847 and sold for many years, but there were several copiers, including Vicars (who produced a variety of needlework accessories) and Woodfield (fig 61a and b). 'The Cornucopia', 1860, was advertised for knitting pins and round netting meshes in sizes 1–24. When the *Dictionary of Needlework*, Caulfield and Saward, was published in 1882, a knitting needle gauge was considered essential for the knitter and the seller of knitting needles. There were over two dozen varieties on the market; a circular gauge with sizes around the edge was in very general use and could be bought, 'at cutlers and wholesaler

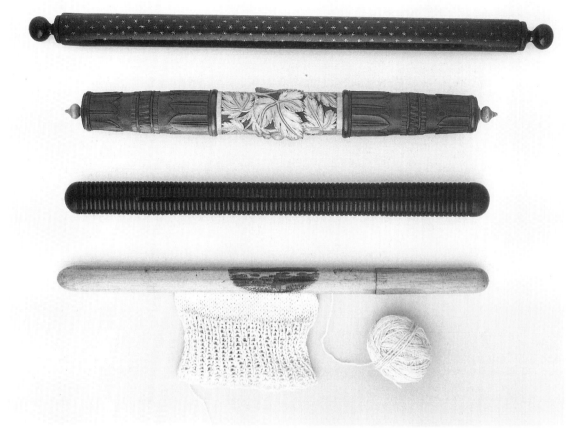

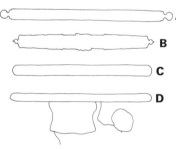

62 *Knitting needle cases, second half of nineteenth century.*
a Wood and papier mâché   b Carved wood, Tyrol
c, d Cases with a slit for the knitting in turned rosewood and
Mauchline Ware

establishments where other materials and articles necessary for the work table are to be procured'. Row counters, either combined with gauges or as single items, were common after 1900. Plastic knitting needle gauges were also made.

Slim wooden cases with a slit in the side held a set of needles in use and allowed the knitting to protrude – they were supposed to prevent dropped stitches but were never very popular. Decorative, cylindrical cases were used to store needles, but they were of limited capacity and may not have been intended for this use exclusively; enthusiastic knitters kept their needles and work in more capacious bags. From the 1880s to the 1930s several manufacturers or wholesalers marketed sets of needles in plain wooden cylinders.

Another device to prevent dropped stitches was a pair of needle

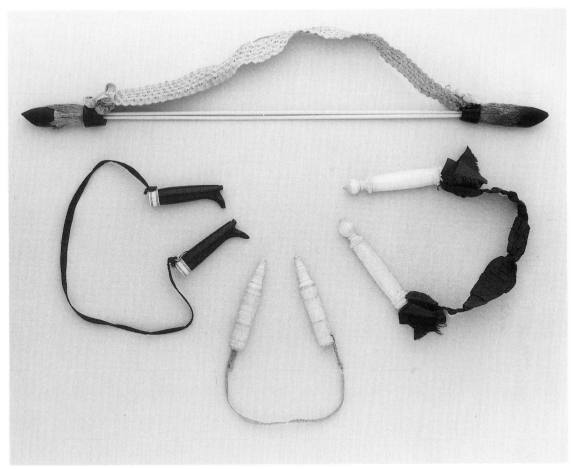

63 *Knitting needle guards, 1880–1910.* *a Plastic and hair*
b Ceramic and bone *c, d Bone*

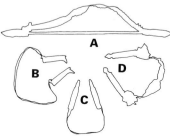

guards or protectors, two caps joined by cord, ribbon, elastic, or a
sliding metal bar which fitted over the points of the needles when the
work was laid aside. Most decorative guards were sold between
1880–1910 for the popular market. Fancy Goods shops and drapers
offered plain and novelty shapes, the majority made in France,
which included imitation hooves (covered in hair), pig's trotters,
ceramic and metal legs and boots, simple beaded cylinders and, after
1900, moulded plastic and painted carved wood. Between 1900–20
serviceable metal protectors were sold with some sets of steel
needles and 'bone knitting pin sheaths joined by elastic' were
advertised by Milwards in 1931.

Until the mid nineteenth century a ball of wool in use could be
prevented from rolling away by keeping it in a wicker cage or in a
wooden bowl turned in a particular shape; those who knitted while
on the move preferred a little bag hanging from the waist. About

1850 the makers of souvenir ware, especially Mauchline, produced spherical holders for knitting wool or crochet cotton to hang from the wrist or a belt. Transfer and Tartan Ware were very popular and also a clever decoration made by covering the complete ball with shaped paper printed to resemble 'scraps' (colour illustrations 6 and 8h). There were similar containers in plastic.

The knitting sheath was a most decorative example of folk art and one of the last forms of traditional carving in Britain. Fine quality sheaths were professionally made in several European countries, but in Britain the majority were hand-carved as a token of love for a sweetheart or relative. 'Sheath' has been preferred to 'stick', since it was used first and continued until the early twentieth century, although in its simplest form a holder could be made from a suitable twig. The average sheath was about 8 in (20cm) long with a hole 1–1½ in (25–38mm) deep bored at the top. It was worn on the right side of the body to hold the right-hand needle and take the weight of the work, which left the fingers free to work rapidly at the points. The majority of sheaths were either tucked into a belt (known as a

64 *Welsh knitting hooks, nineteenth century. One end hooked over a belt, the other supported the weight of knitting. The two largest are made of brass and swivel*, National Museum of Wales (Welsh Folk Museum)

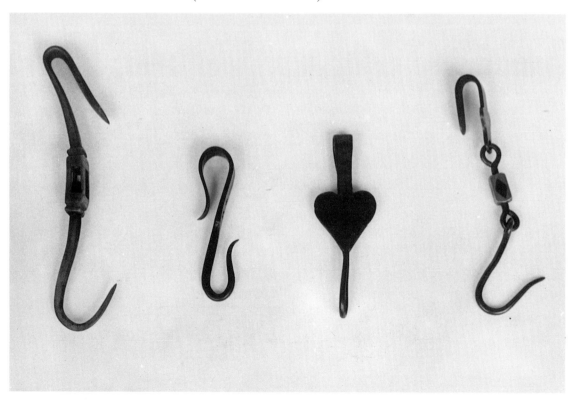

cowband), had an opening through which the belt was threaded, or had a slot to fit over it. Sheaths with diagonal cuts fitted over an apron string, heart shapes were backed with fabric and pinned into position, and a few of the large, so-called 'goosewings' may have been gripped under the arm. Most sheaths were made of wood, but sheet metal, bone, leather and horn were also used. There was a great variety of forms and decorations and, although there were regional shapes, it is rare to find identical designs.

Some writers recorded that knitters used curved needles, but this was the result of constant use – all needles were straight until the introduction of circular steel and plastic ones in the 1920s. William Howitt, in *Rural Life of England* (1844) described the knitters of Dentdale in the West Riding of Yorkshire:

> They knit with crooked pricks and use a knitting sheath
> consisting of a piece of wood as large as the sheath of a
> dagger, curved to the side and fixed to a belt. The women
> of the north sport very curious sheaths made from a wisp of
> straw tied up pretty tightly into which they stick their
> needles, or sometimes a bunch of quills of at least half-a-
> hundred. Upon the band there is a hook, upon which the
> long end of the knitting is suspended that it might not
> dangle.

It is thought that knitting sheaths spread north from Southern

65 *Knitting sheaths from the North of England.*
a Swaledale, Yorkshire   b Teesdale, Durham/Yorkshire
c, f Probably Yorkshire Dales   d No provenance but dated 1934
e Northumberland, York Castle Museum

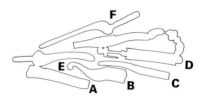

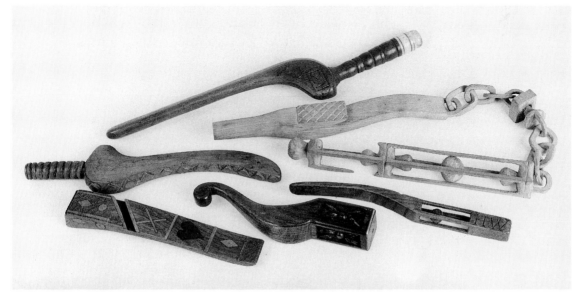

66 *Welsh knitting sheaths.   a Abergavenny   b Pontypridd,*
South Wales   c Cardigan   d Double-ended spindle, Cardigan
e Cardigan, National Museum of Wales (Welsh Folk Museum)

England during the late sixteenth century and were widespread by 1700. Hand knitting, especially stockings, provided suitable relief work for the poor in urban areas, but during the eighteenth century it was forced out of towns by frame-work knitters and only continued in the relatively poor upland areas of Wales, Northern England, the Highlands of Scotland and a few fishing communities around the coast. The stocking frame was invented in 1589 and did not have an immediate effect on hand knitting, but eventually many a shed at the bottom of a garden in the industrial North of England housed a knitting frame for a worker or two. The technique of knitting with a sheath survived until the late nineteenth century, but fell out of use when Education Authorities considered this method was harmful to children's posture and it ceased to be taught.

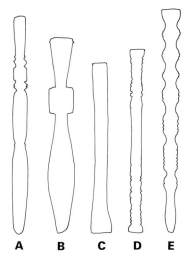

A   B   C   D   E

The first sheaths were probably spindle-shaped, the shape used in Lowland Britain, carved simply to imitate turning. The earliest dated sheath is from 1628, and is in Newarke House Museum, Leicester. After 1850 large numbers were made commercially on lathes in the bobbin mills which supplied textile mills in Northern England; they were used here and in South Wales, where some spindle sheaths were double-ended (fig 66d).

Sheaths with a large, flat-faced blade, more-or-less S-shaped with an upright haft to receive the needle, have recently been described as 'goose-wing'. They were used over a long period, almost exclusively in the Eden Valley, Cumbria and Teesdale and Dentdale, North Yorkshire.

Chain sheaths were elaborate and ingenious. The long chain terminated in a hook to support the weight of the knitting, not the ball (or clew) of wool. The earliest is dated 1680, in Birmingham City Museum, and they continued to be made until this century, the majority in Cumbria, some in North Yorkshire and Wales.

Small, flat, heart-shaped sheaths of wood, leather and occasionally brass were made in Cumbria. Tinplate and sheet brass was popular in West and North Yorkshire, especially around Sunderland. A few were made in the eighteenth century, but the majority, including those of galvanized iron, are much later.

Sheaths of rectangular section with slightly curving hafts, straight cut or scrolled feet, plain or elaborately carved, were made among many knitting communities. Novelties in the form of amusing fish, mermaids, legs and snakes may be the work of sailors along the North-East coast. For a more detailed study of this subject, visits to local museums are recommended, as each area has a comprehensive collection.

CHAPTER 13

Fastenings

Cords

Cords were once essential to fasten clothing, close bags and purses, and to suspend useful articles from the waist – pincushions, pomanders, needlecases, scissors or even handkerchieves. Cords were also couched in intricate patterns to decorate clothing and furnishings.

Cords can be made simply using the fingers to manipulate the

67 *Lucets are very difficult to date but the majority are pre-1830,* York Castle Museum

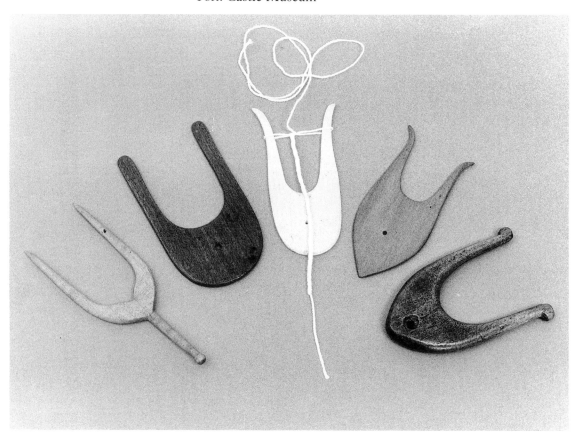

thread, or they can be worked on a small peg-knitting frame (fig 58), but both these methods made a cord that is liable to stretch. In the seventeenth century a small mechanical device was invented to make a miniature three-ply rope, but it was more suitable for a workshop or large household. A fine, though strong, cord could be made easily on a lucet.

During excavations of the Viking settlement at York a broken lucet was found which was easily recognized as the shape has never altered. Lucets were flat and more-or-less lyre-shaped, usually between 3–5 in (75–125mm) in length, with a small hole near the base and sometimes a handle to assist twisting the tool back and forth in use. Cottagers' lucets were made from bone, wood or horn and there were finer tools made of ivory, tortoise-shell and mother-of-pearl. They were in general use until the 1830s but when cheap, machine-made cords became available lucets were no longer necessary. Although ignored by Victorian writers, some rather crude lucets appear to have been made during this period. Lucets are scarce and much sought by collectors; there are a few modern copies.

Most cords were made on the lucet with the fingers, but a curious flat hook about 3 in (75mm) long may have been used by some workers to lift the small loops on to the 'horn'. Printed information about their use is elusive, but occasionally a lucet and hook, made of similar materials, usually bone, are found together. The following instruction for making a lucetted cord is taken from *The History of Needlework Tools and Accessories* by Sylvia Groves:

With the lucet held in the left hand and the ball of thread in the right, the end of the thread was passed through the hole in the base from back to front and secured in position with the left thumb. The thread was brought up at the back of the implement between the horns and wound in front of and then behind the left horn, in the manner of a figure eight, and was then brought out between the two horns. With the right thumb and the forefinger the loop round the right horn was loosened, slipped over the working thread and over the top of the horn, and the loop tightened. The lucet was next turned round in the hand, bringing the right horn forward, from right to left, the thread and knot being pulled across and tightened against what was now the right horn. With the thumb and forefinger of the right hand the loop round this horn was loosened and the process continued as before.

Stilettos

Cords, ribbons and laces were threaded through eyelet holes made with a bone, ivory or metal awl; a stiletto was a small, seventeenth-century Italian dagger which gave its name to the needlework awl, which had a tapered blade and sharp point, and pushed threads apart without cutting them.

Stilettos were made of ivory, bone, silver, steel, mother-of-pearl or wood, or a combination of a steel blade with any of them, including plastic after 1880. Until the early nineteenth century it was common practice to carry a stiletto on one's person and many had a reversible blade or a cap to protect the point. A combined stiletto and needlecase of ivory, in the form of a man's head, has been dated 1780 by the Museum of Costume, Bath; fig 68h also contains a needlecase and may be from a similar date. Elaborately carved ivory stilettos, particularly with a reversible blade, are usually pre-1810. Small tools of silver, silver-gilt and chased steel probably originated in étuis or fitted needlework boxes before 1830. Tools made completely of mother-of-pearl are French pre-1830, or Asian pre-1860, but those with a steel blade and pearl handle were produced throughout the nineteenth century and continued to the 1930s. Undecorated stilettos, especially bone which were made for several centuries, are difficult to date. In 1910 Abel Morrell sold stilettos made of bone and steel with a handle of bone, wood, pearl or erinoid (probably celluloid). In the *Army and Navy Stores Catalogue* (1929), every fitted work basket and case had a steel stiletto with a bone handle.

During the eighteenth century the stiletto was used for a new type of white work embroidery where the pattern was created from a series of holes. At first it was known as eyelet work, but around 1820 this was changed to *Broderie Anglaise*. Although the work could be accomplished entirely by hand, this was rarely done and some of the tedium was removed by printing the design on to the cotton using metal blocks. After 1870 the fabric could be purchased with the holes punched out and only needed to be oversewn to produce the desired effect. However, vast quantities of *Broderie Anglaise* were machine embroidered after 1860; this can be identified from the repeated mechanical precision, especially on the reverse.

Another name for a stiletto was pricker, or piercer, which may be confused with another tool with the same name. Prickers had a very sharp, pointed blade which was not tapered and invariably the blade had a cover, (see fig 68a and colour illustration 12). They were used to prick the patterns for embroidery and lace.

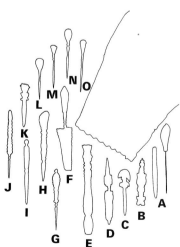

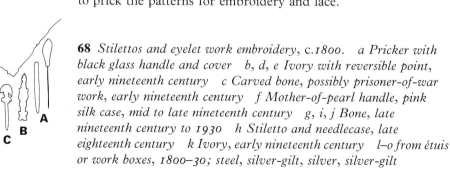

68 *Stilettos and eyelet work embroidery, c.1800. a Pricker with black glass handle and cover   b, d, e Ivory with reversible point, early nineteenth century   c Carved bone, possibly prisoner-of-war work, early nineteenth century   f Mother-of-pearl handle, pink silk case, mid to late nineteenth century   g, i, j Bone, late nineteenth century to 1930   h Stiletto and needlecase, late eighteenth century   k Ivory, early nineteenth century   l–o from étuis or work boxes, 1800–30; steel, silver-gilt, silver, silver-gilt*

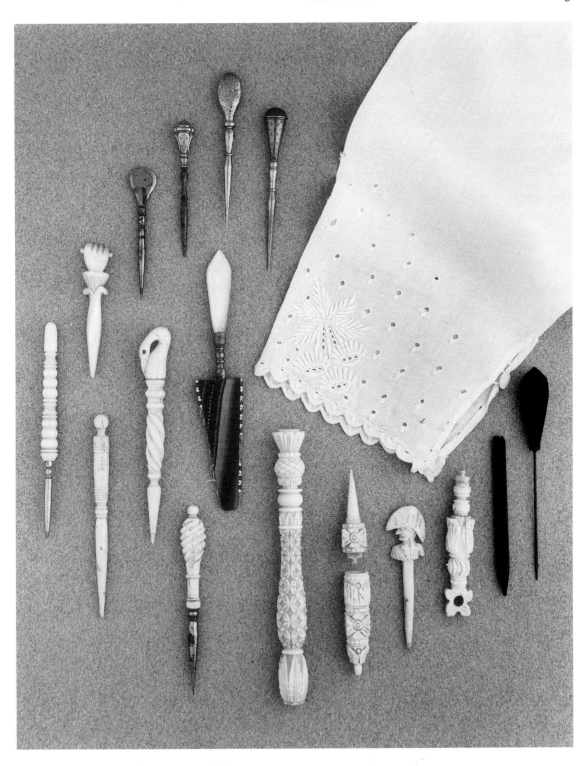

Hooks and eyes

Metal hooks made from round or flat section brass wire, with an eye or worked bar, were introduced in the sixteenth century as an alternative to lacing, by 1638 they were commonplace and cheap enough to be used on the uniforms of boys at Christ's Hospital, 'The Blue Coat School'. Tinned or black japanned steel was preferred in the eighteenth century, and Victorian hooks and eyes were usually, but not always, flat-section; most twentieth-century hooks are round-section plated brass or japanned steel.

From 1800–1900 there were numerous makers. Mr Newey (who bought D.F. Tayler pins) began manufacturing ordinary hooks about 1810 and in 1846 patented the 'Swan hook with a planished bill which gives greater neatness and efficiency'. It was very successful and still manufactured in 1910, when it was used on Queen Mary's Coronation gown. In 1935 Newey's made over 20 varieties of hooks, including one adapted for the new 'Rufflette' curtain tape.

Most packaging was plain and serviceable, consisting of small boxes or cards, but occasionally there were amusing names: 'The Elite', 'The Golf', 'The Tennis' and 'The Ping-pong' were available in 1905.

Very occasionally salesmen's samples have been given to a museum and they are of particular interest, although not always easily dated. In Worthing Museum there is a folder of hooks and eyes which could have been in use between 1880–1910, but these accessories remained unchanged for long periods. There is no indication of the manufacturer, but it is a very comprehensive range with 24 sizes of one design and various others. In contrast, Caulfield and Saward in *Dictionary of Needlework* (1882) only indicated the availability of six sizes, which could be obtained in quantities from a card to half a hundredweight (25.4kg)!

Zips

During the nineteenth century clothes were fastened with laces, buttons, or hooks and eyes, but dressing in fashionable garments needed the assistance of a lady's maid or valet. As people began to have fewer servants, inventors looked for new types of fastening which would be easy but secure.

The first practical design, by Judson, an American, in 1893, was a series of hooks and eyes which were linked together and then opened and closed by the action of a simple slider. It was designed for footwear, but was unsuccessful because the hooks became bent and damaged with repeated use. The rights were sold to another American who formed the 'Automatic Hook and Eye Company', and by the early 1900s a sliding clasp had been developed which linked two rows of identical teeth and worked on the same principle as the modern zip. Optimistically, it was called 'C-Curity', but it failed to live up to its name and was replaced by the 'Plako' which, although trouble-free in operation, was not manufactured successfully until 1913. Many American servicemen came to Britain during the 1914–18 War with clothing and equipment fastened by a zip and in 1919 Kynocks began production in Birmingham. They worked under the same patents, but independently of the Americans, and manufactured the 'Ready' fastener. A separate company was formed in 1924 as Lightning Fasteners Limited (now Optilon).

All zips were made of metal until the mid-1940s although there were experiments with lighter materials; it was not until nylon was introduced that zips became acceptable as a fastening on a wide variety of clothes and equipment. The packaging was always plain.

Press fasteners

These useful accessories were developed in Germany about 1900, but before 1920 most of those sold in Britain came from the area now known as Czechoslovakia. A 1902 catalogue called them 'snap or sew-on dress fasteners', while a 1911 firm preferred 'press studs'. During the 1920s and 1930s various makers, at home and abroad, were producing similar items and the original design of press fastener is still manufactured. The packaging in small card boxes or on cards was always plain.

Buttons

Only inexpensive buttons kept in the work box for repairs are described here.

Hand-made fabric buttons were used over a long period of time but it was the invention in 1840 of a machine for covering a metal disc with fabric, that encouraged manufacturers to set up in business and produce millions of linen buttons. Only the best were covered with linen; other types used cotton, but both were made with or without eyelets. Linen buttons were very cheap but had a short life; many succumbed to the wooden rollers on a mangle and, even if well-made, soon frayed at the edges. They were sold on cards or in boxes containing half-a-dozen to a gross. In 1925 a box of seven dozen assorted sizes cost a shilling (5p). The size, as for most buttons, was determined by lines: one line = one-fortieth of an inch, e.g. 20 lines = half an inch (12.5mm). Eight-line buttons were made for baby clothes, but the majority were 14–36 lines, in two-line increments.

From the 1880s to the late 1930s cards of linen buttons were varied, colourful and imaginative. Some were produced in fancy shapes, for example 'The Fan', 'The Ivy' or 'The Butterfly'. Rectangular cards sometimes carried illustrations of topical events which may help to date them. There were pictures of the Royal

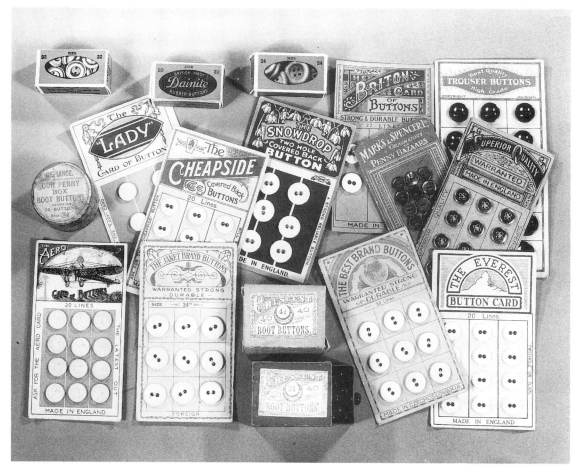

69 *Buttons, 1880–1930*

Family, inventors, liners, aircraft, trains, cars, flowers, birds, well-known people in the news, famous porcelain factories, Gilbert and Sullivan operas and many more.

Small pearl buttons were kept for repairs and were very cheap; in 1920 six dozen could be bought for one shilling and sevenpence (8p). Everyday buttons were made in 12–20 lines and were usually sold on plain cards although a few were decorated – for example a 1902 catalogue had 'The Stag', 'The Crown' and 'The Eagle'. Not all pearls were of the same quality, in fact an 1886 catalogue offered best, seconds, thirds and fourths, each category on a different coloured card for identification. The first imitation pearl button was made in 1904 from casein. It is usually possible to distinguish real pearl from imitation by examining the back: the former may have traces of the rough outer shell, or red or green flecks.

Gentlemen's button boots were introduced in the 1830s and were worn until the 1930s. Ladies' button boots became fashionable in the 1860s but few were worn after 1905. Between 1870–1930 boot buttons were also used on spats and gaiters. The retail trade only sold black, brown and white boot buttons on plain cards or in cheap wooden boxes. The cheapest buttons were made of papier mâché and in 1895 sold wholesale for one shilling and threepence a great gross (6p for 1728!).

From the 1800s metal 'trouser' buttons were used on various items of clothing. They were also sold in wooden boxes and on plain or decorative cards – in 1902 'The As You Like It' had an engraving of Shakespeare.

Rubber buttons will be forever associated with Liberty bodices of the 1920s and 1930s.

CHAPTER 14

Mending

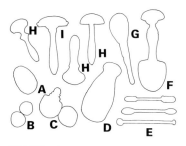

The repair of personal clothing and household linen was not only a necessity: thrift was a virtue. The techniques of patching and darning were already well-known when the darning sampler was

70 *Wooden darners, nineteenth and twentieth centuries.*
a Solid wood egg   b Egg as thimble case   c Mending kit in egg
d Mauchline darning block   e Glove darning sticks
f Sock darner   g Egg on stick, mid twentieth century
h Mushrooms, twentieth century   i Mushroom with spring clip

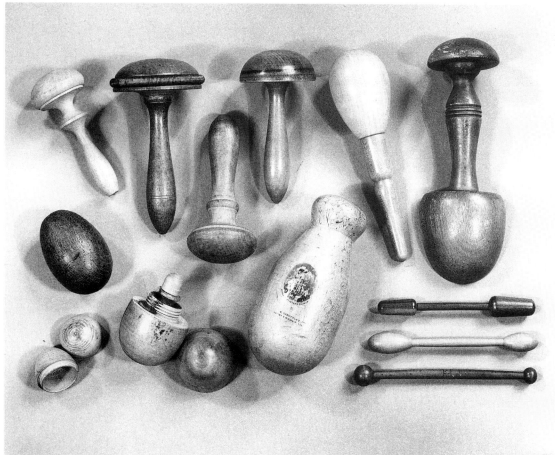

introduced at the end of the eighteenth century, but as this
demanded such a high degree of skill it was not of real practical
value. During the first half of the nineteenth century mending was
not an essential part of education, but from 1870–1930 most girls
were instructed in all the processes necessary to repair garments and
household linen. In 1897 the record book of a student at The Home
and Colonial Training College indicated darning should be taught
in Standard V together with turning the heel of a sock, making
buttonholes and strengthening a placket opening. A few years later
Watson's Soap Works gave away a series of cards about mending
entitled *How to do it – Girls*.

The first accessory to help with darning was probably a wooden
egg. These are difficult to date but the majority are nineteenth
century or later. They were available, but not mentioned, when *The
Workwoman's Guide* was published in 1835; here the worker was
recommended to stretch the material to be darned across her thumb
and forefinger. Eggs varied in size from a pigeon to a goose, and were
either solid wood or hollowed out to hold needles, thread or a
thimble. Not all egg-shaped objects were darners – china, glass,
alabaster and stone eggs were made into hand-coolers for ladies
engaged in delicate white work, who also used sprinklers containing
French chalk to keep their hands dry; pottery eggs were made to
encourage hens to lay. Tiny ivory eggs may have had a useful
purpose, but were probably kept in the display cabinet.

During the second half of the nineteenth century eggs were
largely replaced by darning blocks and mushrooms. The block was
less successful, although the shape was used for souvenir ware, but
the mushroom, in a simple or adapted form, has been made
continuously ever since. The improvements to the basic shape were
either a spring or clip, to secure the fabric while mending, or a small
variation of the shape. The majority have been made this century.
Dark bakelite mushrooms were manufactured between 1900–30,
and bright coloured plastic has been used since the 1940s. There was
a fashion for painted wooden darners in the 1920s and 1930s.

Special darners were made for repairing gloves. A few were
miniature eggs of wood (and ivory?) but the majority were darning
sticks, about 4 in (10cm) long with variously shaped knobs at one or
both ends. Wooden sticks were probably available before 1850 and
were included in Milward's catalogue (1931) at sixteen shillings
(80p) a gross wholesale. Plastic darning sticks were also made.

Darning gadgets were a fertile field for inventors; one even
suggested the work would be a pleasure using his tool! The majority
were made between 1900–50 and many of them must have been
bought on impulse after watching a salesman demonstrating at an
exhibition, only to find they were more difficult to operate than had
been apparent. 'The Marvel Darner' (fig 71e) was a small, polished
wooden holder with numerous short, blunt wires at the end. The
worker was told to: 'Push left hand into garment. Place gripping

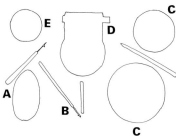

71 *Darning gadgets. a 'The Imra' ladder mender, c.1930*
b The 'Mend-a-Run' ladder mender, c.1940   c Two sizes of the
'Daga' and pin   d The 'Speedweve', c.1950
e 'The Marvel Darner', c.1920

surface on worn part. Turn inside out and darn in the usual way. Never push darner into stocking. Price one shilling.' It was probably made in the 1920s. There were two sizes of 'The Daga' (fig 71c); the grooved wooden block was surrounded by an expanding spring and supplied with a special metal pin: 'Put the part to be repaired over the block and hold in place with the spring. Sew first line of threads as in darning then insert pin under all threads. By a half-twist one way, alternate threads will be raised to facilitate passing the needle and thread across. By rotating the pin the other threads are raised for the next needle run. Price one shilling and sixpence.' The Daga was sold in the early 1930s. The crude 'Speedweve' was made in West Germany after 1945 and used in a similar way (fig 71d).

From the 1920s to 1950s girls could be seen sitting in the windows of dry-cleaners' shops mending ladders in stockings by hand, using a fine hook with a latchet. These hooks could be purchased to do the repairs at home (fig 71b): 'The Ladderkit' was distributed in the

1930s and sold for a shilling, 'The Mend-a-Run Needle' cost sixpence from Etams in the 1940s, at this period a chain of ladies' underwear shops. 'The Imra', probably from the 1930s (fig 71a), was a grooved darning egg with a latchet hook stored inside; in spite of its being patented, 'The Wimberdar' was an exact copy.

It has always been necessary for households to have tools and accessories for emergency repairs when travelling. The exquisite étuis of the eighteenth century and the later 'Lady's Companions' were not always practical, but this hardly mattered as their owners usually had a maid to do the mending. For those that needed a simple, practical container for mending requisites, there was the housewife (or 'hussif') (fig 7g). Some households gave one of these to each young maid when she commenced service. They were made from a length of flannel, calico or printed cotton divided into compartments and stored rolled up and fixed with a tape or button. Commercially-made versions for gentlemen were known as bachelor rolls. Inexpensive small boxes of needlework tools were sold by departmental stores and fancy goods shops after 1880. They were

72 *Lady's Companions in leather cases were made from the mid nineteenth century*, York Castle Museum

not fitted with the best quality tools, but while many were obviously unwanted gifts, others were really practical and well-used. 'The Travelling Companion' (1895) price one shilling (5p), contained pins, needles, thimble, linen and boot buttons, tape, black and white cotton and mending wool.

Very small mending kits were made to carry in a handbag. Some were for stocking repairs only, but from the 1920s small, cylindrical metal and plastic sewing sets were very popular. The lid often doubled as a thimble and there was a multiple bobbin with a few needles inside; tassels were added in the 1930s. The majority were made in Germany, including the moulded plastic shaped as a clown, Dutch girl or soldier (colour illustration 12).

Mending items were one of the few products freely available during the Second World War; sometimes they can be identified by poor packaging and an apology for inferior quality.

Small mending kits are now provided free in some hotel bedrooms. Most of them originate in Hong Kong, but they contain a varied selection of equipment in card or plastic cases.

73 *Child's sewing case and needlework box, Mabel Smorfit's prize, 1903, the charming house probably early to mid nineteenth century,* York Castle Museum

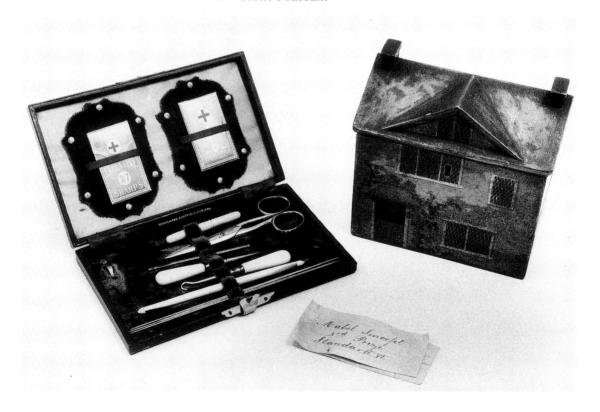

CHAPTER 15

Free gifts

No other trade made more use of the farthing coin than the drapers. From the repeal of the Window Tax in 1845 until 1956, when the farthing ceased to be legal currency, large crowded windows were full of price tickets which included it – 5¾d (said as 'five-three', a farthing less than a sixpenny coin); 11¾d ('eleven-three', just under a shilling); or 19s 11¾d ('nineteen and eleven-three', which seemed so much cheaper than a pound). From 1880–1930 some shops, particulary in the southern half of England, offered a small item of haberdashery, known as 'change goods', in lieu of the farthing change if a customer did not tender the exact money. Shopkeepers made a very small profit if change goods were accepted, as they were

74 *Farthing change goods, 1880–1939*

bought by the gross at a maximum price of two shillings and ninepence, or often much less, whereas a gross of farthings equalled three shillings. 'Black or white sewing cotton on a 50 yard reel at 1s 9d which gives customers satisfaction and shows a splendid profit' (1920). Most change goods can be identified by the printed slogan, 'Your change with thanks'.

Until 1914 there was a great variety of goods packaged for this trade. In 1905 Jeremiah Rotherham & Co. had various types of needles, pin sheets, mixed pins in wooden boxes, button hooks, cards of buttons, mending wool, reels of thread, hooks and eyes and several other lines unconnected with needlework; but, without any doubt, pins were the most popular and outlasted everything else. The cheapest pins were stuck into a very long paper and the shop assistant cut a row off when required. For a little more money, change pins could be pre-packed. In 1902 J. and N. Phillips offered 45 pins in a booklet which could be printed with the name of a shop (incidentally, their penny sheets had 500 pins); a few years later Kirby Beard had change pins in 'concertina fans, shell-shaped booklets and a series of historical scenes in colour which make interesting toys for children'.

75 *Embroidery aids, 1920–39*

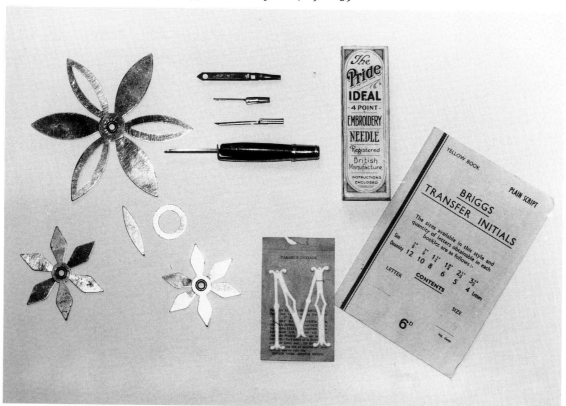

Needles were popular with customers, but the quantity was small. In 1886 Lewis, Wright and Bayliss, makers of 'Cross Fox' brand, offered three needles in a packet and 'Crescent' had five. In 1905 Jeremiah Rotherham listed a single darner with a patent needle threader or packets with such names as 'Russo-Japanese', 'Colonial', 'The Fairy Tale' and 'The Monster'.

Similar items to change goods were used for advertising and may be mistaken for them. Between 1890–1939 some shops included a small gift with a catalogue or calendar; during the same period, but especially in the 1920s and 1930s, needles or pins were fixed to small cards to advertise a particular product and probably given away at exhibitions: Holbrook's Vinegar, Cook's Washing Powder, Edward's Soup and 'Pin Your Faith on Lambert's Tea – it has good points'.

Magazines also gave away free gifts. During the nineteenth century these were restricted to paper patterns for dressmaking or embroidery; the first transfers were not issued until 1911.

For many centuries the accepted way of transferring an embroidery pattern was to 'prick and pounce'. The Stranger's Hall, Norwich, has some 500 embroidery designs, dated 1794–1823, which were copied by this method. The design was traced or drawn on paper and every line perforated with a pricker, either a decorative tool (see fig 68a and colour illustration 12), or a pin or needle held in a pin vice or a cork. Towards the end of the nineteenth century tracing or roulette wheels were useful for long lines. The pricked paper was placed on the fabric, sprinkled with pounce and rubbed through the perforations with a roll of felt or muslin. Pounce was made from powdered French chalk (tailor's chalk, for marking heavy cloth, had been used since the fifteenth century), pipe clay or ground cuttlefish, to which charcoal or a blue pigment could be added for use on light-coloured fabrics. When the paper was removed, the dots of pounce were formed into permanent lines with water-colour paint. *The Dictionary of Needlework* (1882) included instructions for pouncing and how to use carbonized linen paper, purchased in coloured sheets. An American book, *Needlecraft Artistic and Practical* (1889), advertised the use of 'Ingrams Stamping Outfit' for the same purpose.

Meanwhile in 1874 in Manchester, William Briggs, a draper, had patented the invention of a hot iron transfer. He used his family arms as the trademark and in 1886 registered the name 'Penelope'. The manufacture of transfers established this company in the needlework field, and shortly after this they introduced traced linen and simultaneously published their first instruction booklet, *The Manchester School of Needlework*, which became *Needlecraft Practical Journal* in 1900 and *Needlecraft* in 1911, in which the first free transfer was included. For upwards of 30 years Briggs worked closely with J. & P. Coats in the design field and featured these threads in their leaflets and books. In 1963 Coats acquired a

76 *Tracing or roulette wheels were also used in leather work*

controlling interest in Briggs and six years later the Penelope Needlework Packs were launched in self-selection stands. Unfortunately there is no record of the range of Briggs transfers, as everything was destroyed when they were discontinued.

After the lead taken by William Briggs, free transfers were included with many ladies' magazines and in at least two Sunday newspapers in the 1920s – *The Sunday Chronicle* and *The Sunday Graphic*. The majority of designs were very poor, difficult to work, or both; even a *Woman's Day* gift from the 1950s, 'designed by the Queen's dressmaker, Norman Hartnell' was very dull, althouth it did have 'A little reminder – clean hands mean clean work'. The majority of free transfers were dated; pre-1910 examples were usually on stout paper, but the best guide to an approximate date of any transfer is the style of design.

Since the last war, plastic gadgets have been added to the range of free gifts and occasionally a tool for some forgotten craft has been reintroduced – for example, a knave spool for thread, a hairpin for crochet or a peg knitting frame adapted for embroidery.

MUSEUMS

The following museums have needlework tools in their collections and were used as a basis for this book, but the list is not comprehensive; many other museums, and country houses open to the public, have interesting items on show or in store. Most museums do not have everything in their collection on display, and it is advisable to write in advance for permission to see particular collections.

Bath – Museum of Costume
Batley, Yorkshire – Bagshaw Museum
Beamish, Co. Durham –
  North of England Open Air Museum
Bedford Museum
Birmingham City Museum and Art Gallery
Bromsgrove Museum
Cambridge and County Folk Museum
Chertsey Museum, Surrey
Derby Museum
Gloucester Folk Museum
Great Yarmouth – Elizabethan House Museum
Guilford Museum
Honiton, Devon – All Hallows Museum
Leeds – Abbey Museum
Leicester – Wygston's House
Lewes, Sussex – Anne of Cleves House
Lincoln – Museum of Lincolnshire Life
Lisburn Museum, Co. Antrim, Northern Ireland
London – The Victoria and Albert Museum
Luton Museum and Art Gallery

Maidstone Museum and Art Gallery
Manchester – Gallery of English Costume,
  Platt Hall
National Museum of Wales, Welsh Folk Museum
Nottingham – Castle Museum
Norwich – Stranger's Hall
Paisley, Scotland – Museum and Art Gallery
Poole, Dorset – Scalpen's Court
Redditch – National Needle Museum
Salford – Ordsall Hall Museum
Salisbury and South Wiltshire Museum
Sheffield City Museum
Southampton – Tudor House Museum
Skipton, Yorkshire – The Craven Museum
St Albans City Museum
St Helens, Merseyside – Museum and Art Gallery
Stowmarket – Museum of East Anglian Life
Tunbridge Wells – Municipal Museum and
  Art Gallery
Worthing Museum
York – Castle Museum

BIBLIOGRAPHY

'A LADY', *The Workwoman's Guide*, 1836

ADBURGHAM, A., *Shops and Shopping*, George Allen & Unwin, 1964

ANDERE, M., *Old Needlework Tools and Boxes*, David and Charles, 1971

ARNOLD, J., *Patterns of Fashion*

BAKER, J., *Mauchline Ware*, Shire Publications Ltd, 1985

BLAIR, M., *The Paisley Thread*, 1907

BOND, S., *History of Sewing Tools*, Embroiderers' Guild, 1967

BRADFIELD, *Costume in Detail*

BREARS, P.D.C., *The Knitting Sheath*, Folk Life Journal

BUCK, A., *Victorian Costume*, Herbert Jenkins, 1961

CAULFIELD, S.F.A., and SAWARD, B., *The Dictionary of Needlework: An Encyclopedia of Artistic, Plain and Fancy Needlework*, 1882

COLBY, A., *Pincushions*, Batsford, 1952

COURTNEY, C.T., *George Baxter, The Picture Painter*, c.1920

CUNNINGTON, P. and LUCAS, C., *Charity Costumes*, A. & C. Black, 1978

de DILLIMONT, T., *Encyclopedia of Needlework*, D.M.C. Library, 1890

EARNSHAW, P., *The Identification of Lace*, Shire Publications Ltd, 1980

EDWARDS, J., *Bead Embroidery*, Batsford, 1966

FORGE MILL, Needle Museum, Redditch, guide

FRIEDEL, R., *Pioneer Plastic*, 1983

GILL, M.A.V., *Tunbridge Ware*, Shire Publications Ltd, 1985

GROVES, S., *The History of Needlework Tools*, Country Life, 1966

HARDINGHAM, M., *The Illustrated Dictionary of Fabrics*, Studio Vista, 1978

HARVEY, M., *Story of Hand Knitting*, 1985

HIMSWORTH, J.B., *The Story of Cutlery*, 1953

HOLMES, E.F., *Thimbles*, Gill & Macmillan Ltd., 1976
A History of Thimbles, 1986

HOPEWELL, J., *Pillow Lace and Bobbins*, Shire Publications Ltd, 1975

HOVART, V., *Sewing Accessories*, 1980

HUGHES, T., *English Domestic Needlework*, Lutterworth, 1961

JOHNSON, E., *Needlework Tools*, Shire Publications Ltd, 1978
Thimbles, Shire Publications Ltd, 1982

JOSEPH, M., *Introducing Textile Science*

KATZ, S., *Early Plastics*, Shire Publications Ltd, 1986

LEE, B., *The Personal Reminiscences of a Needlemaker*, Merlin Books, 1986

LEVITT, S., *Victorians Unbuttoned*, George Allen & Unwin, 1986

LUNDQUIST, M., *A Book of a Thousand Thimbles*, 1970

LUTON MUSEUM AND ART GALLERY, *Pillow Lace in the East Midlands*, 1958

MORRIS, B., *Victorian Embroidery*, Herbert Jenkins, 1962

PATONS, *The Story of Knitting*

PINTO, E.H., *Treen and Other Bygones*, G. Bell & Sons Ltd, 1969
Tunbridge and Scottish Souvenir Woodware, G. Bell & Sons Ltd, 1970

PROCTOR, M.G., *Victorian Canvas Work: Berlin Wool Work*, Batsford, 1972
Are You Being Served, Madam?, Meresborough, 1987

ROGERS, G.A., *An Illustrated History of Needlework Tools*, John Murray, 1983

RUTT, R., *A History of Hand Knitting*, Batsford, 1987

SMITH, A.K., *Needlework for Student Teachers*, 1894

SWAIN, M., *Ayrshire and Other Whitework*, Shire Publications Ltd, 1982

TYLECOTE, R.F., 'A Contribution to the Metallurgy of 18th- and 19th-Century Brass Pins', *Post-Medieval Archaeology*, Vol. 6, 1972, pp. 183–90

WELDON'S *Encyclopedia of Needlework*, 1886
Practical Needlework, 1936

WHITEHEAD, G., *Old Time Tools and Toys of Needlework*, 1928

WORKWOMAN'S GUIDE, 1835

Index

Figures in *italics* refer to black and white illustrations; figures in **bold** type refer to colour illustrations.